Hope & Spice

Authentic recipes and stories of transformation from the slums of Delhi

Recipe text by Amanda Clegg
Stories by Victoria Byrne

Recipe text by
Amanda Clegg

Stories by
Victoria Byrne

Second Edition 2018

Photography in India
by Amanda Clegg and Victoria Byrne
Food styling in London
by Amanda Clegg and Victoria Byrne
Photography editing and studio shoot: Steve Lee
Photographic assistant: Charlie Lee
Studio Props: Topham Street Styling
Photos of Dr Kiran Martin supplied by Asha
Contributor research: Ayesha Seymour, Asha
Design and layout: Peter Bishop, Banyan Design Ltd

A CIP catalogue record for this book is available from the
British Library
ISBN 978-1-5272-2694-4
Printed and bound in the UK by Amadeus Press
Printed on FSC certified paper

FOR MORE INFORMATION, PLEASE VISIT OUR WEBSITE
HOPEANDSPICE.COM

All profits from this book will go to Asha
Community Health & Development Society via
Friends of Asha (GB).
Friends of Asha (GB) is a UK registered charity 1085071

Contents

Foreword

As Asha is 30 years old this year, I have been reflecting on the 'Asha journey' and how the work has developed since I started it back in the summer of 1988. I would love to take this opportunity to share some highlights with you. That way, if you don't know what we do, or have never visited a slum, you can gain a little bit of background about our charity and context for this wonderful book.

Back in the beginning, in my twenties, I went to medical school and qualified as a paediatrician. I was the only one from my entire batch of 180 medical students who decided to go into the slums. It was a very revolutionary step because it was completely uncharted territory. I started off without understanding what challenges the slums represented, but there was a cholera outbreak at the time in a particular slum and I just knew I had to respond. So Asha's beginnings were very, very small, just me taking a suitcase full of medicines and sitting in a courtyard treating those that came. It was very hot and sultry, it was humid, and I had this burning desire to help these women and children who were suffering so much. There was this huge population of people living in the slums who didn't have any form of access to healthcare. I really felt for them and became determined to set up a professionally run healthcare programme just for them. I wanted to make sure that it would run really well, that it could ultimately be led by the community. It would be a grassroots healthcare programme providing sustainable improvements in the population of the slum. That became my initial goal.

The first step was to train Community Health Volunteers from within the communities themselves. I eventually got some of the women together – it was not easy building trust and getting them to catch the vision. In the beginning they wouldn't even believe they were capable of being trained because at that time they only worked as domestic helps in people's homes. So they could not dream that they could actually act as barefoot doctors, really treat patients and provide valuable life-transforming advice. They started, but at the beginning there were tears, they were shunned, made fun of, ridiculed, partly because they were women. But as time went on, they were able to prove their worth. They showed that they were able to treat illness, to save lives, to help women and children and to help deliver newborn babies safely.

Then I started working in many other slums replicating the model. As I reached out to many other communities, the government began to work with me, and through their intervention and leasing of premises, I established primary care centres in many different slums. Then in 1990 I set up a diagnostic centre because slum patients had absolutely no access to diagnostic services. I began to establish links with various hospitals and other diagnostic centres in the city, creating lots of goodwill so that our doctors could then refer patients for tertiary care in hospital. So that's how I completed the loop: primary, secondary and tertiary healthcare.

Then came women's empowerment. Every time I had discussions with members of the community,

the whole focus was on water and sanitation. At that time, there were no toilet blocks in any of the slums. Women were always talking about how it was such a shameful thing for them to go to the toilet in public, because they had to squat in the park, by an open drain or a railway track. It was too much for me to hear how much shame they had to endure just to go to the toilet. Everyone also kept talking about the desperate need for water, and I could see that it was terrible. The water was muddy, dirty and contaminated with sewage. I started telling them that we have to do something – we can go and approach the authorities and see whether something good can happen out of our actions. In the beginning there was total disbelief that anything would change, but then small successes helped them to understand that this was not impossible. I came to a point where I was able to help these women sit face-to-face with very senior officials and tell them their problems. They made change happen themselves and I am so proud of them. They realised that there was power in their collective action and they became more and more confident in their ability to get the civic services they needed. There were lots of campaigns; there were a lot of struggles along the way but as time went on, the empowerment work really flourished. I set up many Women's Groups and Children's Groups. All

this happened during the '90s, when I also did a lot of primary education work, ensuring the slum children went to school.

Our next focus was to campaign for land rights, which paved the way for the government's land policy and housing policy for people living in the slums. This led to us creating a financial inclusion scheme, whereby slum dwellers could access micro-finance loans for the first time to buy their own land and homes and start businesses. Both were breakthrough initiatives.

Our most recent push, for the last ten years, has been in higher education. In 2008 I personally wrote university applications for the first batch of twenty-five students who were accepted into Delhi University from the slums. Since then, cumulatively, there have been over 2,000 students! Imagine that: I'm blown away! To see them flourishing and accomplishing these things has been unbelievable. They are re-writing their histories and those of their families and their communities.

Over all this time, I'm most proud of the people themselves. I admire their resilience and their courage. I admire their ability to rise from the ashes, their ability to flourish in the midst of some of the

most adverse circumstances in the world. I admire their ability to strive against all odds, against so much opposition, from family members, from society at large, in the face of so many negative messages, so many messages of rejection, so many messages of hopelessness and despair. They've been able to take hold of their lives and offer leadership to their communities and be able to fight for what's rightfully theirs, for a good and decent life. My team have also truly shared this vision. They deeply enter the story of the people, really enter the story of the person concerned. That, to me, is true compassion, when you enter the person's story and you walk with them in that story, rather than just watch from afar.

Now to food. For me, food is not just about eating. Food is about getting together, offering hospitality, strengthening bonds, fostering trust and relationships. Food is about breaking down barriers which God never intended for humanity. It's central to our common humanity together. Food is about celebration, joy. It's about enjoying each other's cultures. Food is about acceptance. It is about love. Food is about validating and affirming people. It's a most wonderful way of bringing people together. In Asha, we like to use every opportunity to celebrate with food. Food has been the most magical way of breaking down caste, in ways that nothing else has done; not collecting water, not having meetings, not distributing blankets, not going to the government offices. None of those things have done what food has done. The moment you are sharing food with people, you immediately say you accept them; you are happy to eat what they have made with their hands. Food is prepared with such love. It is also prepared with sacrifice because some of them don't have much money. So the food they prepare spells love, it spells sacrifice and it spells joy because whatever they have they like to share, to be generous. These are the highest of human values. When you can eat that person's food with a smile on your face and tell them that you care for them, that's all that matters. That happens in the Asha centres but also in people's homes, because hospitality is one of Asha's very important values. Hospitality is about inviting people, it's about sharing whatever you've got. It's about opening up your homes and letting the walls of your homes come alive.

So, to this book. I think this is one of the most

beautiful and special ways of expressing how you can join hearts together across the world. This is a unique way that people from the slums can bring their recipes and share their food with people from all over the world. Imagine the joy they feel knowing others are cooking their food in kitchens far, far away! They are so excited because this is not something that has ever happened before. When they actually see their faces in the book with their recipes there, can you imagine the validation of who they are as people, the kind of affirmation that it gives them? It's just so amazing. I feel that it's going to be such a blessing to you, the reader as well, because you join your heart with somebody. You may not have met that person but it's a joining of the heart, it's a joining of the spirit. There's a very deep and rich experience that both sides can share together as a result of these delicious recipes and touching stories. They are imagining you enjoying their food, and you are thinking about the people who created it and shared it with you, giving them the honour and the respect for the skills they possess.

Thank you so much for buying this book and I sincerely hope you will enjoy it.

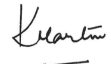

Introduction

It is with enormous pleasure and a heart bursting with joy and gratitude that I want to welcome you to *Hope & Spice*. This book has been the culmination of my ten-year relationship with Asha and the people they serve in the slums of Delhi. 'Asha' means 'hope' in Hindi. The relationship has been life-changing and life-giving for me and I want to share something of that with you, as you start delving into the pages of this book.

My maternal grandmother was born and lived her early life in Calcutta. My paternal grandparents spent their early married life living on an oil field in Assam, where my father was born and lived until he was 7 years old. This Anglo-Indian family heritage contributed to my fascination with India and desire to visit the country that I grew up hearing so much about. My chance came in 2008 when I got the opportunity, through church, to join a group volunteering in the slums of Delhi. That trip was like a light bulb switching on. I loved India from the moment I set foot in her noisy, colourful, dusty streets. But it was her people that really captured

my heart. As I painted that first Asha community centre and met the women and children that used it, I felt a deep connection. Something stirred in me that has never left: a sense that these people are just like me but without my material good fortune. They share the same emotions, the same desire to raise their children well, the same need to find meaning in life and to find creative ways to feed their family; they share the challenges of juggling work and home responsibilities, of being a good citizen in their community. The huge difference is that these women are doing all that in one of the poorest environments on earth. I admire them so much. I hope you will enjoy reading some of their stories – and those of several Asha staff members – and will gain a unique insight into their lives as a result.

Taking many others to work with me in Asha slums over the years has always been eye-opening, enriching, challenging, tiring and enormous fun. Some of the most significant moments have been sitting on a charpoy in a tiny house, hearing a woman tell her story. Sharing these glimpses into their lives has been such a privilege. Listening, learning, laughing, sometimes crying…often while drinking a delicious mug of steaming, gingery masala chai, I have found myself full of respect and admiration for their dignity, resilience, and joy. I have made many friends amongst the community members and the Asha staff and they

now seem almost like extended family to me. I am forever indebted to them for their kindness, their welcome and their patience (I never will nail those Bollywood dance routines!)

Food is a passion of mine, but it is also a necessity for us all. As I thought about this project, I became more and more curious about the sort of food cooked and eaten in the slums. What are their go-to recipes or family favourites? How seasonally do they eat? What food is cooked for celebrations? This project gave me the perfect excuse to find out. Victoria and I visited 12 slum communities and were cooked for by over 100 different cooks – men, women and young people from the slums and from the Asha staff that work with them. This book gives you our carefully curated selection of their food. These are their authentic recipes. We have not anglicised them (other than occasionally using less obscure vegetables). No version is ever definitive either, so you may find alternative recipes elsewhere. We want to give you the delicious food they gave us, it's as simple as that. From time to time we offer shortcuts or variations that we like, but we always flag that up. All recipes have been double tested: cooked by at least one of us and one of our wonderful recipe testers. We really hope you will enjoy making them as much as we have enjoyed bringing them to you.

We have included recipes from Asha's staff, as they help extend variety and showcase some of the more expensive ingredients (especially lamb, chicken and fish) that slum dwellers eat less frequently. The staff serve the communities with incredible compassion and commitment, and regularly share meals with the women in the Asha centres. These are recipes that they cook for the women and some are now Asha favourites. I grew up eating one brown chicken curry served with little bowls of sliced banana, desiccated coconut and sultanas. Good as it was, I have delighted in cooking my way through these recipes and establishing new family favourites of my own. The diversity of flavours and styles is stunning and much better than the rather predictable dishes familiar to us in some UK Indian restaurants.

So, I hope this book encourages you to embark on your own culinary adventure with spice. If cooking Indian food is unfamiliar to you, be brave and give it a go. There are many simple recipes here and we think you'll be pleasantly surprised. Thank you for buying this book. Your support will allow Asha to continue to spread hope amongst those who richly deserve a better future.

Amanda
X.

Tips & Techniques

Indian food does not have to involve lots of ingredients or processes. We have found it much more straightforward than we expected, so we want to encourage you to give it a try, whether you're new to preparing Indian food, or wanting to expand your repertoire. These recipes are varied, reflecting the fact that Delhi is a city fuelled by migration. Some are very simple, some are more involved. Either way, we hope that you will find dishes here that you love. We are thrilled that some of our recipe testers have already adopted their dishes as family favourites. Choose the ones you like the sound of and go from there. We suggest you try these recipes without modifications the first time you make them, except perhaps for the chilli levels (see below). Once you know what the original cook intended, you can tweak them to your taste. Most dishes freeze well and can be cooked ahead to be reheated, so they make great party food.

We thought we'd share some tips and techniques that we learnt both from watching our cooks and from testing the recipes, that we think will give you a head start:

- **Read the recipe all the way through before you start.**

- **Do as much chopping and prep as you can before you actually start cooking.**

- **Don't be afraid of cooking rice! The best rice can be made using the first part of our Lemon Rice recipe; no colander or steamy kitchen needed.**

- **Taste at the end, to ensure the dish is well seasoned and balanced. Add a dash of cream, coconut or sugar to reduce chilli heat or soften spices if needed. Add more chilli if you want to add extra punch, or lemon juice for acidity. Don't be afraid of salt: our cooks often used at least a teaspoon.**

GINGER-GARLIC PASTE

We frequently list this in the ingredients, rather than repeating these instructions in 19 different recipes. Larger UK stores now sell pure, pre-made, frozen cubes of this puree, but you can easily make your own too. If you only need it for one recipe, the tiny amount required is easiest to make by hand. Take equal amounts of root ginger and garlic cloves, peel them; finely grate the ginger, crush the garlic and mix them together.

It's much easier to make a larger batch, in which case use a mini chopper. Puree the equal quantities of peeled ginger and garlic, using some oil if it helps the machine process it. Refrigerate in a screw-top jar or freeze in thin layers or ice-cube trays, well wrapped; use from frozen.

ONIONS

The best tip we learnt from our cooks was how much flavour onions can give when they are really browned. Indian cooks rarely want gently sweated onions. Turn the heat up and cook them for a good 15 or 20 minutes, giving the odd stir, until they reach golden brown or dark brown, as directed. You'll be amazed what umami deliciousness they produce.

CHILLIES

Trust your instincts when deciding what sort of chilli to use and in what quantity. For fresh chillies, our cooks used green ones, and chose thin, relatively hot types (e.g. finger chillies), so we do too. Stick with green ones; they are no spicier than their riper, red version and they give a specific taste. Try slicing off the tip of the chilli to taste it: they vary! The tip is the mildest part; the seeds and inner membranes are the spiciest (and can be removed). These recipes reflect the quantities our cooks used, but if you are not used to chilli try maybe half our amounts. You won't spoil the effect of the dish, since we all have different sensitivities to chilli. A good trick for saucy (curry) dishes is to add chillies whole but pierced and remove them when the dish is spicy enough.

DISH TOO SPICY?

If you need to cool the fire, dairy products such as yoghurt will help, because capsaicin is carried away by oil, not water. Therefore serve a dish of plain yoghurt with your meal. The raitas in this book will do that beautifully.

COOKING WITH YOGHURT

We have found yoghurt can split quite easily, curdling the sauce to which it is added. This won't affect the taste, but will make it look less creamy than was intended. We recommend using full fat yoghurt at room temperature, and adding it gradually to the sauce. Stir constantly at first, until it's incorporated, then it should be fine to bring it the boil.

SHOPPING

We know that not everyone can find fresh curry leaves in their local supermarket. Asian stores, even corner shops, can offer great value for spices, herbs and rice. In supermarkets, the 'World Food' aisle offers much better value on those items than the regular spice/staples aisles. Some of the ingredients lists might seem long, but many of these recipes can be cooked using a limited range of spices. You may be reassured that the same few ingredients turn up frequently in this book:

Coriander seeds   *Coriander leaves*
Cumin seeds   *Garlic and ginger*
Garam masala   *(see above)*
Ground turmeric   *Fresh green chillies*
Red chilli powder   *(see above)*

If you want to expand your options further, go for green cardamom pods. The best plan is to start by shopping for the recipes that appeal and grow your collection over time. If you love spicy coconut dishes you will notice that they are usually cooked with black mustard seeds, dried red chillies and curry leaves, which freeze well. Whole spices can easily be ground in a coffee grinder, which you can clean by processing a piece of dry bread afterwards. Ground spices can burn easily, so watch the heat and stir often; some of our cooks mix a little water into their ground spices before adding them to the pan to prevent them from catching.

MEASUREMENTS

1 teaspoon = 5 ml
1 tablespoon = 3 teaspoons or 15 ml

ONLINE SUGGESTIONS

We can personally recommend www.akaroo.com for dry goods, particularly Indian flours from UK-based Jalpur Millers and www.theasianpantry.com, as well as Amazon.

MEAL PLANNING

The most basic of Indian meals is rice and dal, perhaps with pickle and a raita. An important distinction is that some dishes are saucy (these are the curries) while others are 'dry'. It's best to serve only one saucy element in a meal and choose one or two dry dishes to go with it. Dal can be solid or soupy depending on your preference: just add water. A southern Indian meal, such as our Keralan dishes, would always use rice, whereas northern Indians eat a lot of flatbreads. Some dishes work better with the sweet softness of rice, some with the nuttiness and texture of bread. Have fun!

snacks & light meals

Vegetable pakoras

PREMA, COMMUNITY HEALTH VOLUNTEER AT MAYAPURI SLUM

Prema cooked these crisp-on-the-outside-soft-in-the-middle pakoras for us with such ease. Plates piled high with the different vegetables appeared at speed and we enthusiastically compared them. My favourite was the aubergine, Victoria's was the cauliflower. Prema's daughter likes potato the best, which shows you can use whatever fresh vegetables you have to hand. Prema says this is her favourite comfort food, dipped into homemade chutneys and pickles. She loves to eat them in winter or during the monsoon rains, when she thinks, 'Let's have hot chai and pakoras.' Great as a starter, snack or part of a light meal, you can also use paneer as one of the variants if you want some protein in the mix.

SERVES 4–6

For the batter:
250g gram flour
½ tsp salt
Big pinch ground turmeric
Big pinch red chilli powder
Pinch carom seeds

For the filling:
1 aubergine, cut into long fingers
1 large courgette, cut into
    rounds ½cm thick
½ cauliflower, broken into very
    small florets (2–3cm)
5 large mild green chillies, stems
    removed (deseeded if you
    don't like heat)
2 onions cut in half and into
    thick crescent slices

Vegetable oil for deep frying

First make the batter. Sieve the flour, salt and spices into a medium bowl and gradually whisk in a small cup of water (up to about 200ml), adding it slowly until you have a thick, lump-free batter. It needs to be thick enough to coat the vegetables; thick custard is the benchmark here.

Make the pakoras in batches. Heat the oil in a deep-sided pan (no more than a third full) until really hot. One at a time, dip the vegetable pieces into the batter until they are fully coated, then immediately drop into the hot oil, whereupon they should sizzle instantly. Fry until they are puffed up, crispy and golden brown, then remove with a slotted spoon to a plate covered with kitchen roll. Repeat with the remaining vegetables, keeping the others warm in a low oven or serve immediately.

Great with:

Chutneys and dips, e.g. coriander chutney, tomato chutney or chilli ketchup. Sour cream swirled with sweet chilli sauce would be tasty (if inauthentic).

Bread pakoras

MEENA, COMMUNITY HEALTH VOLUNTEER AT ANNA NAGAR SLUM

When I watched Meena assemble these bread pakoras my first thought was, 'What a lot of carbs!' They are essentially a deep-fried potato sandwich and look extremely filling, which is actually the point. Meena explained that she often cooks them for the children in the Asha kids' group, and that they are always popular as they are hot and tasty. They are inexpensive to make and are actually lighter and fluffier to eat than I expected. Having not been aware of them before we met Meena, we then saw them on sale at many street food stalls around the city. I guess they are the Indian equivalent to a chip butty, but I think much more exciting. Next time you have a crowd to feed, do give them a try.

SERVES 8+

For the batter:
250g gram flour
2 tsp salt
½ tsp bicarbonate of soda
1 tsp ground turmeric
Pinch of red chilli powder
2 pinches carom seeds

For the filling:
1kg potatoes, peeled, boiled and
    mashed
20g fresh coriander leaves
10 thin green chillies, very finely
    chopped (less if you want it
    milder)
Salt to taste
2 pinches carom seeds
1 tsp garam masala

½ packet sliced white bread
Vegetable oil for deep frying

Make the batter. Put the flour, salt, bicarbonate of soda and spices into a medium bowl and gradually whisk in a small cup of water, until you have a smooth batter. It needs to be thick enough to coat the bread, so aim for a pouring custard-like consistency.

Mix the mashed potatoes with the coriander, chillies, spices and salt until evenly blended.

Cut the slices of bread in half into triangles. Take one triangle, top with a generous layer of the potato mixture and add a lid to make a sandwich, pressing it down well. Repeat with the rest of the bread until you have used up all the potato filling. (Cut them in half again if you prefer smaller pakoras.)

Make the pakoras in batches. Heat the oil in a deep-sided pan (no more than one-third full) until really hot. Dip the sandwiches into the batter until they are fully coated, then immediately drop into the hot oil. Fry on each side for 3–4 minutes until they are puffed up, crispy and golden brown, then remove with a slotted spoon to a plate covered with kitchen roll. Repeat with the remaining sandwiches, then serve immediately.

Variation:

For a milder flavour, omit the green chillies altogether or replace with up to 1 teaspoon of red chilli powder. Meena also showed us a bread-free version called Aloo tikki, where she simply battered little balls of the potato mixture. These are great for a lighter, gluten-free alternative, and much quicker to make.

Ramkali, Jeewan Nagar

Ramkali remembers when she first saw Asha's mobile clinic arrive in Jeewan Nagar. She thought they would not last long: 'Most NGOs don't.' Her own life was very restricted: she lived within her own four walls and never went out. 'I was just existing,' she remembers, 'and things were difficult. There were drug problems in the area then.' She would not have felt comfortable talking to a man outside the family, so she couldn't have gone to the police station if she needed to, or talked to a doctor about an ultrasound scan.

It wasn't until her children were sick that she knew things needed to change. She ventured out to Asha's clinic and obtained medicines for them. There she also made friends; she made a connection with Kulwinder who led the work. Ramkali recalls thinking, 'Women are here, it feels good to meet people.' She liked Asha's message of encouragement and undertook three months' training as a Community Health Volunteer. She and

Kulwinder started visiting houses, finding out what people needed. 'My children used to say, "You don't need to roam around the slums. We'll keep you happy at home," but I was stubborn; I wanted to do something outside the house. When I started serving people here at Asha, I was content. Asha has given me an education. I'm really grateful to Dr Kiran for founding this charity.' These days Ramkali loves bringing women together. 'We were nobodies; now we are somebodies. We've learnt that ordinary women can make a difference.'

Ramkali's children have now grown, and it is her five-year-old grandson who poses for our camera as if he already has Bollywood at his feet. Over the years, his grandmother has transformed into a confident woman who knows how to look after her family, and who joyfully shows us how she makes the deep-fried delicacies they serve to Asha's guests. Her fingers have the practised artistry of someone who has made a great many pastries. She seals a delicate pocket of dough to enclose a sweet coconut filling, before she fries it. Following this, she makes the most delicious poppadoms with gram flour, oil and a few spices. We have discovered how much the people of Delhi love flatbreads and poppadoms. The women of this slum are showing us how it is done and we are mesmerised. Ramkali deftly rolls out the spice-speckled dough into a paper-thin disc. Lifted from the board, it is translucent, tan, perfectly round and cross-hatched from the ridges of her special rolling pin. She flips it into a little karhai of hot oil and within half a minute I am crunching the spicy, savoury treat.

Ramkali is delighted we like them. 'I will make some for you tonight to take back to your husbands,' she says. When we meet Kulwinder the next day, we are presented with two piles of wrapped poppadoms. Unfortunately, our husbands are over 4,000 miles away, and we fear the crisp and exceptionally tasty treats will not travel well. They are delicious.

Spiced poppadoms

RAMKALI, COMMUNITY HEALTH VOLUNTEER AT JEEWAN NAGAR SLUM

Whenever I go to a curry house in the UK, we always start with poppadoms and chutney. I love breaking them into crisp, jagged mouthfuls, topping them with mango chutney, lime pickle or mint chutney. I had never considered making them until I saw Ramkali at work. Not only did she make them look very easy, but her spice-enriched dough produced the most beautiful crispy, flavoursome poppadoms you can imagine. She used a delicately ridged, wooden rolling pin to create the thin, almost translucent, discs. Victoria and I commented on it, only to find that a few days later two rolling pins were pressed into our hands by an intermediary: Ramkali had sent for some from her village by special request. Now I have no excuse not to make my own, but let me reassure you that a standard rolling pin will work just fine. You won't get the pretty cross-hatches but you will still produce stunning fresh flavour and crunch.

SERVES 4

200g gram flour
½ tsp salt
½ tsp red chilli powder
½ tsp carom seeds (or cumin
    seeds if you haven't got them)
Pinch of asafoetida (if you have it)
Vegetable oil for deep frying

Chutneys and pickles for serving

Put the flour, salt, and spices into a medium-sized bowl or electric mixer and gradually stir in enough water to form a thick, firm, dry dough. Tip it onto a floured work surface and knead for 2–3 minutes until it is smooth. Cover the bowl with a damp tea towel or cling film whilst you make each poppadom.

Tear off a walnut-sized piece of dough and form it into a small patty. Place on a surface such as a wooden board (lightly oiled to prevent it from sticking) and roll into a very thin disc (ideally no more than 1mm thick). Set aside and repeat with the rest of the dough.

Heat around 5cm depth of vegetable oil in a deep-sided pan until very hot. Lower in a poppadom and deep fry for a few seconds until it has puffed up, bubbles have appeared on the surface and it is golden and totally crisp. Repeat with the other rolled-out discs, transferring the cooked poppadoms to a warm plate or oven as you go.

Serve immediately with chutneys, pickles or very finely diced vegetables. Store any leftovers in an airtight container and eat within a day or two.

Great with:

Chutneys and dips, e.g. coriander chutney, tomato or tamarind chutney or chilli ketchup. Sour cream swirled with sweet chilli sauce would be tasty (if inauthentic) if you haven't any Indian condiments to hand. Add diced red onion, tomato or cucumber for a more substantial topping.

Spiced scrambled eggs

AZAD, ASHA STAFF AT PEERA GARHI SLUM

Azad has been working at Peera Garhi slum for two and a half years, under the leadership of David, making it (unusually) a male staff team. Having been raised in Zakhira slum himself, and attended the children's group there, he knows first hand what is it like to experience the support and educational opportunities that Asha offer. How wonderful that he is now passing these on to a new generation of children. These scrambled eggs piqued with chilli are a regular breakfast staple for Azad, who smiled broadly as he extolled their virtues: cheap, quick and tasty. Why not also try them for brunch or lunch, maybe with some hot, buttered toast on the side?

SERVES 2

4 eggs
1 medium onion, finely
    chopped
1–3 thin green chillies, very
    finely chopped
Salt and pepper to taste
1 tbsp coriander, finely chopped
2 tbsp vegetable oil

Break the eggs into a roomy mixing bowl and stir with a fork until the yolks and whites are combined. Add all the other ingredients and mix well.

Put a pan over a medium heat and add the vegetable oil. Once it is warm, tip in the eggs and stir gently with a wooden spoon until they are scrambled to your liking. Serve immediately.

Variation:

I habitually order masala eggs in India and they often come with finely chopped tomato in addition to the onion and chilli. Feel free to experiment according to what is at hand; a sprinkling of toasted cumin seeds is also an excellent addition.

Sometimes I like to fry the onion and chillies first, before adding the eggs, if I want a softer texture or have a hankering for a deeper fried-onion flavour.

Paneer bhurji

SHIV, ASHA STAFF AT SEELAMPUR SLUM

I first met Shiv in 2010 when he was a teenager living with his family in one of the labyrinthine lanes of Seelampur slum. He made an immediate impression on me with his sunny smile and stunning Bollywood dance moves. Since then, all with the expert guidance and support of Asha, he has completed his schooling, gone to university and secured a job. Shiv now works for Asha in several slums, teaching and mentoring the next generation of children. Although he is not really a cook, he wanted Victoria and I to visit his home and took the opportunity, with the help of his sister, Anita, to prepare this delicious, quick and easy dish for us. Fresh, colourful and tasty, I highly recommend it as a light lunch or snack on its own, with any Indian bread or even on toast.

SERVES 2

150g–175g paneer (Indian cheese)

2 tbsp vegetable oil

1 tsp cumin seeds

1 tsp fenugreek seeds

1 medium to large onion, chopped

1 thin green chilli, finely chopped

2 medium tomatoes, roughly chopped

½ tsp garam masala

½ tsp ground coriander

Pinch red chilli powder

¼ tsp ground turmeric

Salt to taste

Fresh coriander, to garnish

First, to give shop-bought chilled paneer the lovely softness of homemade Indian paneer: crumble or grate it, then soak it in a bowl of boiling water for 2–5 minutes until soft and springy. Drain well and set aside.

Heat the oil in a frying pan, and when it is really hot, add the cumin and fenugreek seeds. Let them sizzle for a minute, then add the chopped onion. Fry, stirring well until it is tinged golden brown at the edges. Add the chopped green chilli and tomato, garam masala, ground coriander, red chilli powder, turmeric and salt. Stir well and cook over a medium heat until the tomato is soft.

Add the paneer and cook, stirring gently for a couple of minutes, until it is amalgamated and hot throughout. Check for seasoning then garnish with fresh coriander and serve immediately.

Variation:

Shiv and Anita used crumbled fresh paneer and their dish resembled scrambled eggs. Meera at Chanderpuri slum also cooked this for us but she used larger 1cm cubes of paneer, which gave the dish a chunkier texture. Interestingly, she used half the tomatoes and omitted the garam masala and ground coriander, so feel free to experiment!

Zubair, Seelampur

Weaving through Chandni Chowk, possibly the busiest street in Delhi, we knew we were in safe hands because Zubair was guiding us through the crowds. He's a young man with a wise head on his shoulders. We made sure to keep his smart shirt and upright figure in our sights as the people, cars and tuk-tuks roared around us. Later I sat with him in Asha Seelampur's peaceful courtyard to hear about his involvement with the charity.

Zubair grew up in Seelampur with his six siblings; his parents run a vegetable stall and he saw the long hours and very hard work it required. He keenly remembers the injustice of a policeman hitting his father instead of asking him to move on. He hoped for a better life for his family, and was interested when he heard about Asha. He took the opportunity for extra English classes with their volunteers. English is one of India's official languages, so it's an important step into a good job.

With Asha's encouragement he stayed in school and university, graduating in political science with honours. Asha opened a door for him to an internship with The Lodhi, a top luxury hotel in Delhi, and they liked him so much they offered him a job, with a golden handshake. He is now able to earn more than four times the wage of his parents, who are very proud of him.

I asked him about his role at The Lodhi. He explained that he supervises housekeeping, checking the rooms and liaising with the reception staff. Not very long ago he was doing his school work. Now he is managing a staff of 27. To celebrate Diwali, the hotel sent a car to deliver a bouquet and a hamper of sweet treats to his parents. He was very proud that his work could bless his parents as they had supported him. He has big dreams to help them. 'I want to give my parents a beautiful house out of the slum in a few years' time,' he explains. It would be a big change from the very small house in which they have brought up seven children. It's not just a pipe dream.

Zubair is only 24 but he has learned how to save his hard-earned money and invest it fruitfully. He has already started two businesses, including a factory which his cousin and brother run. Asha has given him teaching, education support and medical care (among other things) but he has seized every opportunity with courage and hard work. He's also aware that it is not a solo effort. He particularly credits the encouragement of his Asha friends including Shiv and Subodh, Asha Seelampur's Team Leader for many years until recently. Just a few years of investment in Zubair have borne fruit that blesses him and all those around him.

Kathi roll

ZUBAIR, STUDENT AMBASSADOR AT SEELAMPUR SLUM

I have known Zubair well for the last 5 years and over that time I have seen him blossom into such a successful young man, yet his achievements haven't turned his head. Not only is he saving to buy a house for his parents outside the slum, he is also 'paying it forward' by mentoring the younger students coming up through the Asha support system on his days off. What a fantastic role model! His job in the seven-star Lodhi Hotel means that he has access to modern interpretations of Indian dishes that would be quite unknown to his own family. When he heard we were coming to Seelampur, he went to see the chef and asked to be taught how to make this popular dish. He was so thrilled to pass it on to us. Originating from Kolkata, kathi rolls are common street food all over India and make a great light meal. A bit like an Indian fajita, they are quick to make, endlessly versatile and deliver exciting layers of contrasting texture and flavour.

SERVES 1

For chicken filling:
2–3 tbsp vegetable oil or butter
1 medium onion, finely
    chopped
2 tsp ginger-garlic paste (see
    page 10)
1/3 red pepper, finely chopped
1 cooked chicken breast, cut
    or shredded into very
    thin slices
Up to 1/2 tsp red chilli powder
Salt

For kathi roll:
1 fresh or ready-made
    paratha or chapatti (or
    any flatbread or wrap)
Mayonnaise
Coriander chutney (see p160)
1/2 small red onion, finely sliced
Paneer (Indian cheese),
    to grate (optional, or
    replace with mozzarella)
Fresh coriander leaves

Start by making the chicken filling. Heat the vegetable oil or butter in a medium-sized frying pan until hot. Add the chopped onion and fry until soft and golden. Turn the heat down, add the ginger-garlic paste and red pepper and fry, stirring well until the red pepper is also soft. Add the shredded chicken, chilli powder, salt and mix well. Cook for 3–4 minutes over a gentle heat until the mixture is warmed through. Set aside on a plate, and wipe the pan clean with kitchen roll.

Take your chapatti or flatbread and warm it for a minute or two in the same frying pan. Put it on a plate and spread with a very thin layer of mayonnaise. Lay your onion slices and fresh coriander down the middle and top with the hot chicken mixture. Drizzle the filling with the coriander chutney and grate some paneer on top. Roll up the chapatti to form a cylindrical wrap, securing it with a cocktail stick if needed. Cut in half on the diagonal and serve straight away, with kitchen roll or napkins at hand to catch any juicy drips!

Variation:

Replace the chicken with mixed peppers and cubes of paneer for a vegetarian alternative.

chicken

Chicken korma

SHASHI, ASHA TEAM LEADER, SEELAMPUR SLUM

Shashi is famous for her chicken korma and her eyes twinkle as she proudly tells us it's her signature dish. She makes it for her family on Sundays and has been known to cook three kilos of it for an Asha team meeting. In the UK, korma tends to denote a sweet, yellow curry that is often the entry-level dish for people trying Indian food, or for those who don't like chilli. In India, kormas tend not to be sweet and vary much more in heat level and colour. Some use nuts, coconut or poppy seeds in the sauce and most have a dairy component. Shashi's delicious version is characterised by plentiful onions cooked until really brown and sweet, and a sauce made from natural yoghurt. It contains no chilli or nuts, so is still a good choice for those who prefer mild curries. She uses chicken pieces on the bone, but feel free to use boneless thighs if you prefer.

SERVES 5–6

4–5 tbsp vegetable oil
400g onions, finely sliced
900g skinless chicken pieces
    (thighs and drumsticks)
3 tsp ginger-garlic paste (see page 10)
2–3 tsp ground coriander
2–3 tsp ground cumin
1½ tsp garam masala, plus more
    for sprinkling
Salt to taste
Freshly ground black pepper
200g full-fat natural yoghurt (not
    Greek style)
Fresh coriander to garnish

Heat the oil in a large lidded pan or casserole dish over a medium heat then add the sliced onions. Cook, stirring from time to time, until they soften and turn translucent then golden then dark brown. It is this caramelisation that adds flavour to the dish, so don't be tempted to move on too soon.

Turn up the heat further then add the chicken pieces and fry until sealed and golden. Add the ginger-garlic paste, fry for 1 minute, then add all the spices and season generously with salt and freshly ground black pepper. Mix well and cook the spices for 1–2 minutes to develop their flavour. Turn down the heat, add the yoghurt gradually, a spoonful or two at a time, stirring really well after each addition to form a creamy sauce. Have patience here, as it may curdle if you add it too quickly or don't stir it well enough. Cover the pan and let the chicken braise for 30 minutes until it is cooked through. Add a splash of water if needed or if you want a runnier sauce.

When ready to serve, sprinkle with extra garam masala, garnish with plenty of fresh coriander and serve with rice.

Variation

Try blending 50g chopped cashew nuts or almonds with enough water to form a smooth paste. Add this along with the spices for a richer, more Mughal-style sauce.

Amritsari fried chicken

VIDYA, ASHA STAFF AT MAYAPURI SLUM

Vidya is warm and welcoming and it is lovely to see her again after a few years. Her laugh is infectious, and she immediately puts us at our ease, as she bustles around the kitchen area in the Asha centre in Mayapuri, getting ready for the day of cooking ahead. She explains that she enjoys this fried chicken either with coriander or tamarind chutney as a snack, or with rice and dal as a main meal. She grins as she says she chose it because she knows it's delicious, she is confident making it and it is always popular with western volunteers. She is quite right: these gently spiced chicken pieces are crispy on the outside and succulent in the middle. Serve as Vidya would, or pile it into pitta bread with shredded salad, mango chutney and raita for a quick, tasty, juices-dripping-down-your-chin meal.

SERVES 4

500g skinless boneless chicken, cubed
Juice of ½ lemon
2 tsp ginger-garlic paste (see page 10)
Large pinch ground turmeric
Large pinch red chilli powder
¼ tsp ground coriander
¼ tsp ground cumin
¼ tsp garam masala
Salt to taste
Plenty of ground black pepper
200ml vegetable oil for frying

Put the chicken pieces in a bowl with the lemon juice, ginger-garlic paste and all the dry spices. Season well with salt and pepper, stir to combine, cover with cling film and leave to marinate for 1 hour in the fridge.

In a karhai or frying pan, heat the vegetable oil until hot. Tip in the chicken mixture, then stir fry until the chicken is golden, crispy at the edges and cooked through. Serve hot.

Dr Kiran Martin

The first time I meet Dr Kiran I am with people whom I do not know well. We expect a quick chat with this busy lady. Instead, she sits with us for over an hour and asks each one of us what inspired us to come to Delhi. She laughs and claps with joy when something delights her; she is warm and genuinely interested in us. She is insightful in her responses to us, in a way that helps each of us appreciate our unique gifts.

In subsequent meetings with Dr Kiran, it is clear what a 'people person' she is. She clearly loves face-to-face contact with her staff, volunteers and beneficiaries of the charity. She and her husband

Freddy most like to do this by hosting people for meals around their generous dining table. Regular staff meetings always end with a shared meal because they recognise the impact of eating together. One evening we have the privilege of being fellow guests with Dr Kiran's five mentees. These are students and young professionals who have received Asha's help and are now finding their way in higher education and the business world. The evening is full of fun and they clearly love and respect Dr Kiran and Freddy and are relaxed in their company. She gives them space to talk about the challenges they are currently working on and champions their successes, which are impressive. She is politically aware and hugely knowledgeable, yet she is also quick to put everyone at their ease. She has a gift for conversation and her emotional intelligence seems to bring out the best in us all.

Dinner at the Martin home is fascinating for Amanda and I, because Dr Kiran and Freddy enjoy sharing their appreciation and knowledge of the food with us. In doing so they reveal illuminating things about Indian life.

Their food is delicious, but what strikes me most that evening is the loving respect and attention given to each guest. I can see that Dr Kiran's mentees feel the same way as I do: that spending time with her builds you up so you feel more capable and truer to yourself. Then, when you leave, you are treated to one of her famous hugs. She treats you as your sister or auntie: essentially, you are family. This is a refrain we hear a lot, because Dr Kiran's wholehearted integrity has been embedded in all that Asha does.

Coconut chicken

DR KIRAN, FOUNDER AND DIRECTOR OF ASHA

Dr Kiran adores cooking and loves having people around her table, eating, chatting and laughing together. Victoria and I were completely spoilt by her as she produced one delicious meal after another, having carefully planned them for our enjoyment. This gorgeous mild chicken dish is one of her favourite creations and we can see why: tender chicken in a smooth, creamy tomato and coconut sauce is both moreish and comforting. Simple to make, it can be prepared ahead of time and gently reheated when needed. A family favourite in the Martin household, we think this will soon become one in yours too. Great with rice and a fried vegetable accompaniment.

SERVES 6

3 tbsp vegetable oil
¼ tsp black mustard seeds
8–10 curry leaves, torn into
   large pieces
1 medium onion, finely chopped
2 heaped tsp ginger-garlic paste
   (see page 10)
3 large tomatoes, finely chopped
½ tsp red chilli powder
¾ tsp ground turmeric
1½ tsp garam masala
Salt to taste
1kg boneless chicken thighs,
   chopped into smallish chunks
8 tbsp coconut milk powder or
   1 x 400ml tin coconut milk
Fresh coriander to garnish

Heat the oil in a karhai or large pan, add the mustard seeds and stir until they pop. Add the curry leaves, stir fry for 30 seconds, then add the chopped onions and cook until they soften and turn golden. Add the ginger-garlic paste, fry for 1–2 minutes, then tip in the chopped tomatoes. Stir well then add the chilli powder, turmeric, garam masala and salt to taste. Mix well, adding a splash of water to create a masala paste and cook over a medium heat for 3–4 minutes to develop the flavour.

Increase the heat, then add the chicken pieces, turning them over to brown and get evenly coated in the spice paste. Turn the heat down, cover the pan and cook for 5 minutes until the chicken has changed colour.

Mix the coconut milk powder in a jug with a little water to make a smooth paste, then dilute with a further 350ml–400ml water to a milk-like consistency. Add this (or the tinned coconut milk) to the chicken. Bring to the boil, check the seasoning and simmer until the chicken is cooked through and the sauce is smooth and creamy.

Garnish with fresh coriander and serve with rice.

Aromatic chicken curry

LAXMI, ASHA STAFF MEMBER AT KALKAJI SLUM

Laxmi gave the impression of being a very calm, confident and experienced cook as she talked us through this recipe. Don't be put off by the long ingredients list: the method is straightforward and all the different spices combine to make a lovely masala blend. It tastes rich, aromatic and absolutely delicious. Laxmi often eats it on its own with rice, chapatti or naan to mop up the tasty sauce. If she wants to make more of the meal, she also serves a dry vegetable dish such as aloo gobi, and adds a splash of rosewater to the chicken at the end of cooking for extra fragrance. Since this contains no cream, yoghurt or coconut milk, this is a good choice if you want a lighter curry that still delivers bags of flavour. Laxmi made this with chicken pieces on the bone, but we have used boneless thigh meat for ease.

SERVES 4

2 tsp ground coriander
¼ tsp red chilli powder
¼ tsp ground turmeric
¼ tsp garam masala, plus extra
    for sprinkling
3–4 tbsp vegetable or coconut
    oil
10–12 black peppercorns
2 green cardamom pods
2 black cardamom pods (if you
    have them)
2 big bay leaves
2 x 5cm cinnamon sticks
2 medium onions, chopped
25g root ginger, peeled and
    grated
50g garlic, peeled and minced
2–3 medium tomatoes, finely
    chopped
500g boneless chicken thighs,
    chopped into chunks
Salt to taste
Fresh coriander to garnish

Mix all the dry spice powders together in a small bowl with just enough water to form a thin paste. Heat the oil in a karhai or large lidded pan over a medium heat. Add the peppercorns, cardamom pods, bay leaves and cinnamon sticks and fry for a minute or two until aromatic. Add the chopped onions and cook until they soften and turn golden. Add the grated ginger and minced garlic, fry for 1–2 minutes, then tip in the chopped tomatoes. Stir well and cook until they start to disintegrate. Add the spice paste and cook over a medium heat for 5–6 minutes to develop the flavour.

Increase the heat then add the chicken pieces, turning them over to brown and get evenly coated in the spice mixture. Add enough water to form a sauce, turn the heat down, cover the pan and simmer for 10–15 minutes or until the chicken is cooked through.

When ready to serve, sprinkle with extra garam masala, garnish with fresh coriander and serve with rice or bread.

Keralan coconut chicken curry

THRESSI, TEAM LEADER AT MAYAPURI SLUM

Thressi originates from southern India, but has worked for Asha in Delhi for decades now. Mayapuri is in the east of the city and is a long, thin slum that stretches for 2 km along the edges of a railway track and a huge metal scrap yard. It is a dirty, noisy, industrial neighbourhood and an extremely challenging place to live. The Asha centre is a beacon of hope and calm in the midst of chaos. Thressi commutes four hours each day to work there. She runs the operation with warmth, kindness and authority. I took my first team of volunteers there in 2009 so Mayapuri and Thressi will always be special to me. This dish tastes fresh and aromatic with the ginger, curry leaves and mustard seeds. The coconut milk brings a creamy smoothness to these flavours and the fresh coconut pieces add crunch. Thressi says that back home in Kerala she would eat this from earthenware plates topped with banana leaves.

SERVES 4–5

2–4 thin green chillies
50g or 5–6cm root ginger, peeled and roughly chopped
40g or 8–10 large garlic cloves, peeled
2–3 tbsp coconut oil
2 medium onions, chopped
1 tsp ground turmeric
3 tsp ground coriander
1½ tsp red chilli powder
2 tsp salt
Plenty of ground black pepper
10–12 curry leaves, torn into large pieces
¼ fresh coconut (or 1 x 110g snack pot of coconut chunks) cut into very thin slices
750g boneless chicken thighs, chopped into chunks
1 x 400ml tin coconut milk
½ tsp black mustard seeds

Put the green chillies, root ginger and garlic into a food processor or blender, and whizz to a rough paste. Heat the coconut oil in a large, lidded pan, then add the mustard seeds and fry until they pop. Add the ginger-garlic-chilli mixture, the onions, powdered spices, and salt and pepper. Fry for a couple of minutes then add the curry leaves and coconut slices and stir fry for 30 seconds.

Add the chicken pieces, mix well; add four tablespoons of water, then cook until the chicken turns opaque. Add the thick cream of the coconut milk and stir well. If more sauce is wanted, add the runny coconut milk as well (or just use half or a whole tin if yours does not have distinct layers). Cover and simmer over a low heat for 15–20 minutes, stirring halfway through, until the chicken is cooked through. Serve hot with rice.

Chicken biryani

RAZDA, MEMBER OF WOMEN'S GROUP AT SEELAMPUR SLUM

Biryanis have always seemed slightly mysterious and magical to me. Layers of rice and fragrant meat with a golden drizzle of saffron are sealed together in a pot to cook as one. Some biryanis are even encased with a thick pastry lid, creating culinary theatre as they are pierced with a spoon, letting out amazing, perfumed steam. However Razda's version was not complicated. I am now a convert to making them at home; they are a great choice to prepare ahead of time and cook in the oven until your guests arrive. Razda's green bangles chinked as she finished her dish with saffron colouring – as she said she couldn't afford the real thing. You may prefer to drizzle the saffron liquid over the dish after assembly but before cooking, or do as she does and use it as an aromatic finishing touch.

SERVES 6

500g basmati rice, soaked in cold water for an hour

3 tbsp vegetable oil or ghee

1 tsp cumin seeds

8–10 black peppercorns

1 cinnamon stick, broken in half

3–4 cloves

3 green cardamom pods, bruised

1 black cardamom pod (if you have it)

1 bayleaf

2 heaped tsp ginger-garlic paste (see page 10)

3–4 thin green chillies, sliced longways

2 medium onions, finely chopped

6–8 cloves of garlic, finely chopped

2–3 tbsp natural yoghurt

Salt to taste

850g boneless chicken thighs, chopped into smallish chunks

3 tbsp milk

Pinch saffron strands

Optional rosewater, crispy fried onions and toasted pistachios to garnish

Drain the rice from its soaking liquid and parboil in a large pan of salted boiling water for 5–6 minutes until the grains are soft on the edges but firm in the middle. Drain and set aside.

Heat two tablespoons of the oil in a karhai or large pan, add the cumin seeds and stir until they sizzle. Add all the other spices and stir fry for 30 seconds, then add the ginger-garlic paste and the chillies. Fry for 1–2 minutes, then tip in the chopped onions and garlic and fry them until they are soft and golden brown. Turn the heat down a bit, spoon in the yoghurt gradually, stirring well as you do so. Add salt to taste, then add the chicken pieces and fry until opaque and almost cooked through. Add a quarter of a cup of water and stir well; you want some sauce to be clinging to the chicken pieces.

Warm the milk, take it off the heat and infuse the saffron in it whilst you assemble the dish.

Pre-heat the oven to 180°C, fan 160°C, gas mark 4. Take a casserole dish or lidded cooking pot. Put it on a low heat with a spoonful of oil or melted ghee in the bottom. Put in a third of the rice, level it off then add half of the chicken, then repeat. Finish with the last layer of rice and smooth it flat. Drizzle over the saffron flavoured milk and another tablespoonful of melted ghee or butter but do not stir it. Cover with a close-fitting lid and cook in the oven for 20–30 minutes until the rice grains have separated and absorbed all the flavours. Serve hot, perhaps garnished with a few drops of rosewater, crispy fried onions and/or toasted pistachios.

lamb

Lamb tikki

SHAHZADI, STUDENT AT ZAKHIRA SLUM

These lamb tikki were a joy to discover, just like Shahzadi who cooked them for us. Her lovely smile lit up the room as she talked about her life and ambition: she is relishing doing a degree in political science and aspires to be a politician. For now, she lives with her parents and four siblings in their small, neat two-room home. Taught to cook these by her mother, she made them with goat mince, but they are equally delicious with lamb. Crisp and crunchy on the outside and soft in the middle, these moreish tikki burst with the fresh, clean flavours of chilli, ginger and coriander. Serve as a light meal with flatbreads, chopped spring onions and cucumber, raita and chutneys, or as part of an evening meal with a vegetable dish, dal and rice or bread.

SERVES 4, as part of a meal

250g lamb mince
100g chana dal, soaked overnight or for 2 hours minimum
2 dried red chillies, very finely crumbled
6–7 garlic cloves, finely chopped
¼ tsp ground black pepper
Salt to taste
½ red onion, very finely chopped
1 thin green chilli, very finely chopped (optional)
2–3cm root ginger, peeled and grated
1 tbsp fresh coriander, roughly chopped
1 egg
1 tbsp gram flour or cornflour
3 tbsp vegetable oil for frying

Put the lamb mince in a mixing bowl with the drained chana dal, crumbled red chilli, chopped garlic and salt and pepper. Mix together well, then leave for 10–15 minutes for the flavours to develop. Put the mixture in a small pan, add about 110–130 ml of water and cook over a medium heat until it comes to the boil. Turn the heat down, partially cover and cook for 20–30 minutes until the lamb and lentils are soft and the water has evaporated. You are aiming for a dry mixture. Take off the heat.

Add the chopped onion, green chilli, ginger and fresh coriander to the pan and combine well, working the mixture hard until it is completely homogeneous and the meat is well mashed (this helps it bind together). Add the beaten egg and flour and mix well. Oil your palms, then shape the mixture into small, round, flattish patties about 6cm across. Ideally refrigerate them for 30–60 minutes or longer, as it will help them firm up and handle better. Take a frying pan and heat the vegetable oil until hot. Add the tikki and fry until they are crisp and golden brown on both sides, turning them over (very gently) halfway through to ensure they are evenly cooked. Serve piping hot.

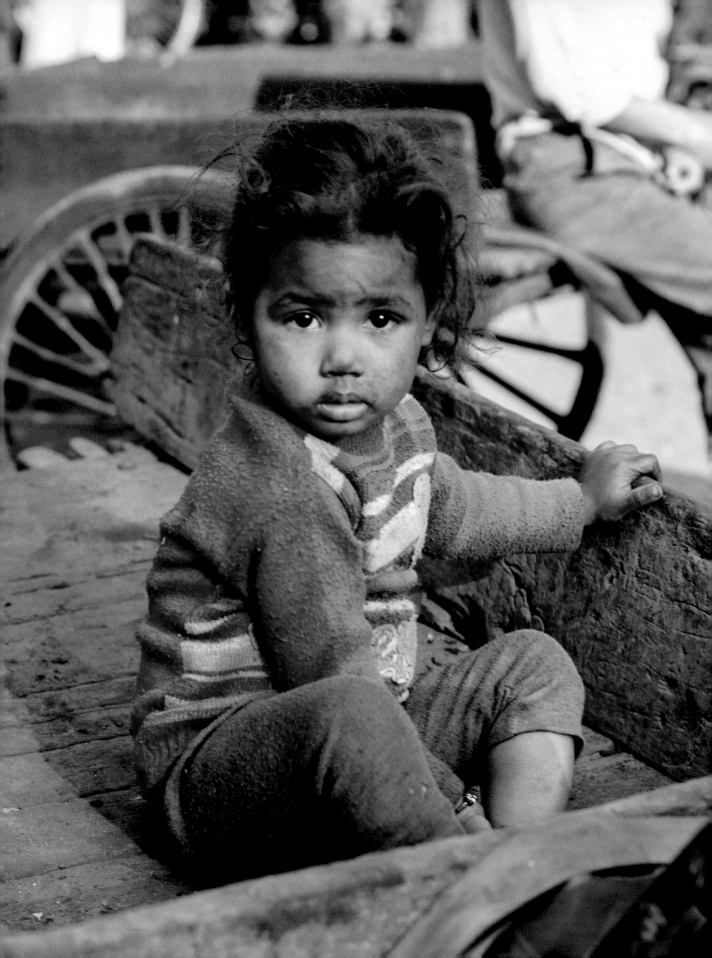

Rihana, Peera Garhi

Rihana's eyes shine with welcome and she's the first to give us strangers a big hug. When the children run into Peera Garhi's Asha centre they make a beeline for Rihana; her sweet nature makes her easy to trust.

She brings us a plate of aromatic shami kebabs and enjoys our appreciation of her cooking. She first came to Asha seeking help at a desperate time. She had lost her husband, and after that there was no-one in her family who could assist her. She went door to door but found few people able to help. When she hadn't eaten for three days she finally arrived in tears at her community's Asha centre and they welcomed her in, gave her sandals, something to eat, and were able to give her a job cleaning their building.

When David the team leader saw what good work she did, and the way she talked to people, he gave her a chance to train as a Community Health Volunteer, a role in which she can significantly improve the quality of life for residents of Peera Garhi. It's now two years on from those terrible days. She wipes her eyes as she describes how Asha rescued her. She clearly values the people around her, and reaches out a hand to touch her colleague's arm as they tell us how they love her kindness and calm.

Rihana is responsible for helping young children in the slum and encourages their families to make use of Asha's services. She co-ordinates the children's group, and we're told she is never without a child at her side. 'The parents always let the kids come because they trust her: it's all about relationship.' Rihana loves to share her food, having learnt to cook from her father and grandfather, who were chefs in America. But really she's all about the children. As she starts telling us how much she enjoys being with the little ones, her face breaks into a big smile. 'Now I'm able to help others,' she says, 'it gives me satisfaction. I feel like myself. Asha is my family.'

Lamb shami kebabs

RIHANA, COMMUNITY HEALTH VOLUNTEER AT PEERA GARHI SLUM

These shami kebabs are Rihana's favourite dish, and she delights in telling us how to make them. Whilst they appear similar to the lamb tikki, there are two important distinctions that make for a very different eating experience: firstly, the mixture for these is ground to a smooth paste; secondly the generous quantity of garam masala gives a rich, aromatic flavour of cinnamon, cardamom and cloves. Rihana works the mixture by hand on a traditional grindstone, as they would have done in Lucknow, 'the kebab city,' where this originated; we have used a food processor. Traditionally, these are loved for their velvety-smooth texture and super-spicy kick, but feel free to reduce the quantity of chillies to suit you.

SERVES 4–6

500g lamb mince
200g chana dal, pre-soaked in cold water for an hour
4 dried red chillies, very finely crumbled
5–6 garlic cloves, very finely chopped
2 small red onions, very finely chopped
1–4 thin green chillies, very finely chopped
4–5cm root ginger, peeled and finely grated
Small handful fresh coriander, finely chopped
1 tbsp garam masala
1 egg, lightly beaten
3 tbsp cornflour or gram flour
Salt to taste
3 tbsp vegetable oil, for frying

Put the lamb mince in a pan with the chana dal, add water to just cover the meat and cook over a medium heat until it comes to the boil. Simmer for 20–30 minutes until the lentils are soft and the water mostly evaporated; you are aiming for a dryish mixture. Take it off the heat and let it cool for a few minutes. Tip into a food processor or blender and grind well until you have a completely smooth, thick paste, or mash in a pestle and mortar. Put this in the fridge to cool down, and continue once the mixture is cold. This makes it easier to work with as it helps the kebabs hold together.

Add all the other ingredients and combine well, working the mixture hard until it is completely homogeneous. Oil your palms, then shape the mixture into round, flattish patties about 5–6cm across. Take a frying pan and heat the vegetable oil in it until hot. Fry the kebabs in batches until they are golden brown on both sides, turning them over halfway through to ensure they are evenly cooked. Add more oil if necessary to prevent them sticking. Serve piping hot.

Great with:

Chapattis or parathas, coriander or mint chutney and some cooling raita. Finely sliced onions and a drizzle of fresh lime juice are also delicious accompaniments.

Variation:

Some recipes add all the ingredients except the green chillies, coriander, egg and flour to the lamb mince at the beginning. This means they are cooked and ground together giving an even smoother texture to the kebabs. Add the remaining ingredients once the mixture is cooled and proceed as above.

Lamb with spinach

RANI, SUPERVISOR OF MULTIPLE ASHA SLUM TEAMS

I have known Rani for 10 years and whenever I am around her she always inspires me. She has been working at Asha for 28 years and has an aura of quiet authority about her. Rani is passionate about women's empowerment and loves seeing women in the slums transition from feeling isolated and voiceless to being agents of change in their families and community, through Asha's intervention. She is also a fabulous cook and we share a love of good food and colourful earrings! This warming lamb dish is stunning – full of deep, complex flavours that are very moreish and satisfying.

SERVES 6–8

3 large red onions, finely chopped
3–4 tbsp vegetable oil
1kg diced shoulder of lamb
2 tbsp ginger-garlic paste (see page 10)
2 tbsp ground coriander
2 tsp ground cumin
2 tsp red chilli powder
½ tsp ground turmeric
1 tsp garam masala
6–7 ripe tomatoes or 1 x 400g tin peeled plum tomatoes
Salt to taste
500g fresh baby spinach, chopped (or frozen chopped leaf spinach)

Fry the onions in the vegetable oil in a large pan over a high heat. As they start to colour turn the heat down and cook them slowly for 10 minutes until really soft and well coloured. Turn the heat up again and add the lamb, in batches if necessary, frying it until browned. Remove the lamb and onions to a bowl and set aside.

In the same pan, add another spoonful of oil if needed, then over a medium heat stir in the ginger-garlic paste and all the spices. Blitz the fresh or tinned tomatoes in a blender, then add to the pan and stir well. Fry the mixture for at least 15 minutes to develop the flavour of the masala mix and give a thick, puree-like consistency, adding a spoonful or two of water if needed.

Add the onions and lamb back into the pan, with salt to taste and enough water to form a thick sauce. Bring to the boil and then simmer, covered, for 45–60 minutes until the lamb is really tender and the sauce has reduced further. Add the fresh or frozen spinach and cook, uncovered, on a low heat for 20–30 minutes, stirring from time to time, until the sauce is thick and any water that has come out of the spinach has evaporated. Check the seasoning, then serve hot with rice or chapattis and some optional mint raita on the side.

Variation

As with *muttar paneer*, I prefer to briefly cook the spinach (with 2–3 tablespoons water) then puree it in a blender before mixing it into the cooked lamb. It creates a lovely, thick, bright green sauce.

Kashmiri lamb yakhni

SHABNAM, ASHA COMMUNICATIONS TEAM MEMBER

Shabnam is really proud of her Kashmiri heritage and enthusiastically describes the stunning beauty of the mountains, the crystal clear air and the wazwan cuisine. These are traditional dishes prepared for weddings and feasts, featuring upwards of twelve meat dishes. Lamb yakhni is one of them, and what makes it unique is its pale, almost white, sauce made with yoghurt. Uncharacteristically, it contains no chilli or turmeric, staples of both Indian and Kashmiri food. This dish is loved by Shabnam and her mother, who always makes it for Christmas and family gatherings. The meat is meltingly soft, the sauce gently fragrant and creamy and the flavour improves the next day, making it a great option to prepare ahead. It is always served with rice, to mop up the thin sauce.

SERVES 6

1kg lamb, ideally shoulder, cut into medium-sized chunks
1 tbsp fennel seeds, ground to a powder
3 green cardamom pods, lightly crushed
2 black cardamom pods (if you have them)
Pinch ground ginger
1 cinnamon stick, broken into pieces
3 tbsp vegetable oil
1 large onion, thinly sliced
¼ tsp cumin seeds
3 cloves garlic, chopped
1 egg
1kg thick plain yoghurt (not low-fat)
Salt to taste

Put the lamb in a large, lidded pan with the ground fennel, cardamoms, ground ginger and cinnamon stick. Add just enough water to cover the meat and mix well. Bring to the boil, then turn down the heat, cover the pan and simmer for 20–30 minutes until the lamb is tender. Set aside.

Put a large saucepan or fireproof casserole dish over a medium heat, add 2 tablespoons of the oil and when it is hot add the sliced onion and cumin seeds. Cook slowly until the onions are golden, then add the garlic. Continue cooking until the onions are dark brown. Turn off the heat and let the pan cool a little. Meanwhile, whisk together in a bowl the egg, the remaining tablespoon of vegetable oil and the yoghurt until smooth.

Put the onions back on a medium heat and add the yoghurt mixture very slowly, stirring continuously, as it is incorporated. Strain the lamb, keeping the cooking water but discarding the whole spices. Add the meat and some of the cooking liquid (300–600ml) to the yoghurt to get a thinnish sauce (adding as much or as little as you want to get your preferred consistency). Cook for 15–20 minutes, adding salt to taste, until the sauce is creamy and the meat meltingly soft. Serve hot with plain, fluffy rice to mop up the delicious sauce.

Variation:

Add 2 bay leaves and 3–4 cloves with the other spices when cooking the lamb.

Lamb kofta

Pinky clearly loves to cook: she came to the Asha centre not with one dish, but bearing a tray of three of her favourite meat dishes, with a pile of handkerchief-thin breads to accompany them. She explained that she is a self-taught cook who loves feeding her family and getting their praise. She cooks from scratch for ten people each day and they typically eat meat around four days a week, an unusually high frequency for the people we met. Her food was incredibly good and this meltingly tender meatball dish was our highlight. She made it with goat mince, but lamb or even beef works just as well.

SERVES 4

500g lamb mince
1 medium red onion, very finely chopped
2–3 thin green chillies, very finely chopped
Handful of coriander leaves and stems, finely chopped
¼ tsp of garam masala
Salt to taste
4 tbsp vegetable oil
4 tbsp ginger-garlic paste (see page 10)
4 tsp ground coriander
1 tsp red chilli powder
Coriander leaves to garnish (optional)

First make the kofta or meatballs. Put the lamb mince in a mixing bowl with the finely chopped onion, green chilli and fresh chopped coriander. Add the garam masala and salt to taste. Mix together well, then shape firmly into egg-shaped balls.

Take a large frying pan and heat the vegetable oil in it until hot. Add the meatballs and fry them until they are lightly browned all over, turning them gently so they don't disintegrate. Remove them with a slotted spoon and set aside. Turn the heat off.

In a small bowl, mix together the ginger-garlic paste, ground coriander and chilli powder, adding salt to taste. Using the same pan, put it back on a low heat and add the paste mixture. Fry it until the spices are fragrant and paste is cooked, maybe 2–3 minutes, stirring frequently to avoid it burning. Add a glass of water to the pan to create a sauce, bring it to the boil, then carefully lower the meatballs back into the pan. Simmer gently for 10 minutes until the meatballs are cooked through.

Sprinkle with fresh coriander and serve hot with rice or chapattis.

Nargisi kofta

PARVEEN, COMMUNITY HEALTH VOLUNTEER AT SEELAMPUR SLUM

Parveen explained that this exotic dish has been handed down the generations in her family, who came from Meerut in northern India. A Muslim dish, *nargis* means 'daffodil' in Urdu and kofta means meatballs. Named because of their surprising yellow centre – each meatball contains half a hard-boiled egg – this is a wonderful example of lavish Mughlai cooking. A show-stopper of a dish, this is a little time-consuming to make, but it is totally worth it when you want to make something that no-one here is likely to have tasted before.

SERVES 4

For the kofta:
400g lamb mince
2 tbsp gram flour or plain flour
1 tsp couscous
Half a small onion, very finely chopped
2 thin green chillies, finely chopped
3cm root ginger, peeled and grated
¼ tsp red chilli powder
1–2 stalks of coriander leaves, finely chopped
2 hard-boiled eggs, cut in half
¼ tsp salt

For the sauce:
3–4 tbsp vegetable oil
2 medium onions, thinly sliced
1 black cardamom (if you have it)
2–3 green cardamom pods
12 black peppercorns
Small shard of cinnamon stick
2–3 cloves
2 tsp ginger-garlic paste (see page 10)
1½ tsp red chilli powder
1½ tsp ground coriander
¼ tsp salt
100g plain full-fat yoghurt
Chopped coriander leaves to garnish

First make the kofta. Put the lamb mince in a food processor with all the other kofta ingredients except the eggs, and pulse until they form an even mixture. If you have time, put the mixture in a covered bowl in the fridge for 30 minutes (or even overnight). This will help it firm up and make the meatballs more robust, but it is not essential.

Make the sauce. Take a large, deep-sided frying pan and heat the vegetable oil until hot. Add the onion slices and fry over a medium heat until they are a really rich brown colour. Remove with a slotted spoon and set aside. Add the whole spices to the pan and stir until they are fragrant. Mix the ginger-garlic paste, powdered spices and salt with enough water to make a thin paste, then add that to the pan. Add the yoghurt a spoon at a time, stirring really well all the while, until it is all incorporated. Turn the heat down and let it gently bubble away whilst you form the kofta.

Take a quarter of the meat mixture and flatten it against your palm to make a curved patty. Place half an egg in the centre, then press the meat around it to form a ball (similar to a scotch egg). Add the softened onions back into the sauce, then carefully lower in the meatballs. Add a splash of water if needed, then simmer gently for 20–30 minutes until they are brown and cooked through. Sprinkle with coriander leaves and serve hot with chapattis to mop up the creamy, aromatic sauce.

Variation

This method makes very large kofta. I would consider cutting the eggs into quarters and encasing those, or using quails' eggs instead to make the end result smaller. Some recipes deep fry the kofta before adding them to the sauce. Fry them for 5–6 minutes until golden brown all over then remove and drain on a plate covered with kitchen paper. Add them to the sauce and reduce the cooking time to 10 minutes, or until everything is piping hot.

Raan

FREDDY MARTIN, ASSOCIATE DIRECTOR OF ASHA

Freddy loves to cook so when Victoria and I stayed with the Martins, he cooked some really delicious dishes for us in the evenings. This was a particular highlight that Freddy liked so much he cooked it twice. It is an Indian spiced, roasted leg of mutton but lamb also works a treat. Restaurants cook it in a tandoor, but a regular oven – which of course no slum dweller has – gives great results. The secret of this dish is the long (overnight) marinade, which tenderises the meat and infuses it with flavour. It's great as an alternative Sunday roast with some spiced roast potatoes, or cook it on the BBQ in the summer for an extra smokey flavour, served with naan and mint raita.

SERVES 6–8

1 leg of lamb
Juice of 2 large limes
250g plain yoghurt
1 tbsp ground turmeric
2 tbsp red chilli powder,
    Kashmiri if you have it
1 tsp ground black pepper
500ml pineapple juice

Put the lamb on a board and cut deep incisions into the meat all over the joint, but especially in the thickest part. Rub the lime juice into the meat and leave it whilst you make the marinade.

In a bowl, mix the yoghurt with the spices until evenly blended. Massage this mixture into the meat, using your fingers to ensure it penetrates deep into the slashes and the whole joint is covered. Leave for 2 hours, covered, in the fridge.

Transfer the meat to an ovenproof dish and pour the pineapple juice over the meat, turning it over so both sides get coated in juice. Cover with cling film and put in the fridge overnight. In the morning, turn the joint again, so the other side of the meat sits in the juice.

Pre-heat the oven to 200°C/180°C fan/gas 6. Put the dish in the centre of the oven and roast for 45 minutes. Turn the joint over and cook for another 45 minutes. If it is browning too much, then cover with tin foil but it is supposed to have some dark patches. Check the meat is cooked to your liking (I like it pink, but if you prefer it well done give it longer), then leave it to rest covered with tin foil for at least 10 minutes. Carve into thick, juicy slices and serve immediately.

Variation:

Add 2 teaspoons of ginger-garlic paste and a tablespoon of garam masala if you want a more deeply aromatic marinade. You can also slow cook this in a cooler oven (180°C/160°C fan/gas 4) for 2½ hours, covered with tin foil for the first couple of hours, if you prefer.

fish & seafood

Prawn malai curry

ANWESHA, ASHA COMMUNICATIONS TEAM MEMBER

Anwesha explained that this is a favourite Bengali dish that she learnt to cook from her grandmother, who came to Assam in India during partition. There she used sweet freshwater prawns from the great Brahmaputra river. Anwesha told us that this is traditionally the first solid meal cooked for babies when they start the weaning process: girls at 6 months and boys at 9 months. They are given the deliciously nutritious coconut sauce and rice while the parents eat the prawns. It sounds infinitely preferable to our baby rice and rusks! Anwesha's grandmother's signature dish is an absolute winner: plump juicy prawns in a creamy glowing red sauce with a warming boost of chilli.

SERVES 4

20 large raw prawns, peeled or 400g medium king prawns
2 medium onions, very finely chopped
2 tsp ground coriander
2 tsp red chilli powder (Kashmiri if you can get it)
3 tbsp butter or ghee
2 tsp ginger-garlic paste (see page 10)
2 thin green chillies, very finely chopped (optional)
1 x 400ml tin coconut milk
Salt to taste
Pinch of sugar
Fresh coriander and a sprinkle of garam masala to garnish

Place the prawns in a bowl with 1 teaspoon of the chopped onion, 1 teaspoon of the ground coriander, and 1 teaspoon of the red chilli powder. Mix well and leave covered with cling film for 30 minutes.

Heat the butter or ghee in a karhai or frying pan over a medium heat until melted. Flash fry the prawns for 1 minute until they have just turned pink on the outside. Remove with a slotted spoon and set aside.

On a medium heat, add the remaining onions to the pan with the ginger-garlic paste, green chillies and the remaining ground coriander and red chilli powder. Stir well and cook this masala mix until it is brown, being careful not to let it catch on the bottom. When you see the butter separating out, sprinkle in a few teaspoons of water and repeat the process until the masala is really aromatic and well developed.

Add the prawns, coconut milk, salt and sugar and stir gently to combine. Add half a cup of water, bring to a simmer on a low heat and cook for 5–10 minutes until the prawns are cooked through and the sauce has reduced slightly to a delicious, creamy gravy.

Sprinkle with fresh coriander and garam masala (if desired) and serve immediately with rice.

Variation:
Reduce the chilli powder and or omit the green chillies if you prefer milder dishes.

Shainy, Zakhira

Shainy grew up in Kerala, a beautiful coastal state famed for its landscape and the food it produces: fish straight from the sea, enjoyed in aromatic dishes fragrant with curry leaves, chilli and velvety coconut milk. Shainy trained there as a pharmacist, but jobs were scarce so in early adulthood she moved 1,600 miles away to Delhi. It even meant adopting a different language for her daily life: instead of Malayalam, she now had to work in Hindi. All this has given her a deep appreciation for the way people in Asha treat each other with love, as family.

Rani was like a mother to her, training her when she first joined the charity, teaching her to lead a team. We ask Shainy what sustains her in facing the many social issues affecting the community. 'It's seeing the changes in people's lives,' she explains, and she runs through the impressive statistics of what Asha has achieved just in Zakhira. There has been a massive reduction in the incidence of TB, vitamin deficiency and malnourishment. Asha has greatly improved safe childbirth thanks to community training and hospital referrals and they have also been instrumental in increasing school participation from 30% to 90%.

Local people used to feel helpless to make changes, but Shainy's team has shown them how to meet their own collective needs, including by lobbying local government. The community now has basic toilet facilities, electricity and drainage. Local government representatives have also discovered that if they make people's lives better, they win votes. Shainy is even happy that her own team has become smaller since residents themselves now fill the roles that were first

modelled by staff and the initial transformation work has been completed.

Shainy's eyes really light up when she talks about the people she's close to. 'I visit my Keralan family once a year, but I also find [Asha founders] Dr Kiran and Freddy are very loving and supportive.' These days as she walks through the lanes of the slum, she has an air of calm, quiet authority. She has matured into someone the children look up to as a role model, who has shown them that doors can be opened. Walking around the lanes with her today, we see many people smile hello. The children all call her *Didi* which means 'big sister'.

Keralan fried fish

SHAINY, TEAM LEADER AT ZAKHIRA SLUM

This simple but delicious fish dish was a daily staple for Shainy when she lived in coastal Kerala in southern India. Now that she lives inland in Delhi, she explained that she cooks it a little less often, but it is still part of her repertoire of recipes that are quick to prepare after work. Fish is generally so speedy to cook – all this needs is a little marinating to really get the flavours humming and then you can have dinner on the table in moments. I have used salmon here, but feel free to experiment with other firm fish; the only stipulation is that it should be really fresh to get the best flavour and most succulent texture.

SERVES 3–4

2 tsp ginger-garlic paste (see page 10)
1 tsp red chilli powder (Kashmiri if available)
¼ tsp ground turmeric
½ tsp salt
500g fresh salmon or 3–4 fillets cut into large chunks
3 tbsp coconut oil (or vegetable oil)

Optional:
Lime wedges to serve

In a bowl, mix together the ginger-garlic paste with the spices and salt. Coat the fish with the mixture and leave to one side for at least 30 minutes or longer if you have time, so the flavours can permeate the fish.

Heat the oil in a frying pan until hot and fry the fish over a high heat, turning it once, until it is just cooked through and the flesh has become opaque. Be careful not to overdo it, or the fish will lose its soft succulence.

Serve immediately with rice and with lime wedges to squeeze over if you have them.

Fish curry

SHALINI, TEAM LEADER AT EKTA VIHAR SLUM

It was the middle Saturday of our time in Delhi and I arrived at the Asha polyclinic next to Ekta Vihar slum feeling rather jaded after a wonderful, but non-stop, week of watching, listening, writing and eating. Shalini appeared looking smiley and serene with two freshly made dishes ready for us to taste: her special fish curry and cumin rice. It was the first fish we had eaten so far, and the bold, fresh and zingy flavours were just what I needed to reinvigorate me. Shalini explained that she loves to cook this on a Sunday for her family, when she has time to enjoy preparing it and they can all sit down to share it together. This Bengali dish normally uses mustard oil for a distinctive, tangy flavour. Instead, we have used vegetable oil and doubled the mustard seeds.

SERVES 3–4

500g fresh white fish e.g. cod, halibut, or monkfish cleaned and cut into large chunks
1 tsp ground turmeric
Salt to taste
10 cloves garlic, peeled
10g root ginger, peeled
½ tsp black mustard seeds
2 medium tomatoes, chopped
5–6 tbsp vegetable oil
¼ tsp cumin seeds
2 dried red chillies
2 medium onions, finely chopped
½ tsp red chilli powder
½ tsp garam masala
Fresh coriander to garnish

Sprinkle the fish pieces with ½ teaspoon of the turmeric and ½ teaspoon salt and leave to absorb for 15 minutes. In a mini chopper or food processor make the garlic, ginger and mustard seeds into a paste. Scrape this out onto a plate and then grind the tomatoes to a pulp. Set aside.

Put a frying pan, karhai or saute pan over a high heat and add 5 tablespoons oil. When it is hot, turn the heat down to medium and quickly fry the fish in batches until it is sealed on the outside and golden brown. You are not cooking it through at this stage, so just a minute or two on each side should do. Remove to a plate lined with kitchen roll to absorb any excess oil.

Add another tablespoon of oil to the pan if the fish has absorbed most of it; heat it up until hot, then add the cumin seeds and dried red chillies. Let them sizzle for a minute or two, then turn the heat down to medium and add the onions. Fry until golden then add the ginger-garlic-mustard paste, stir well for a minute or two, then add the tomato pulp. Mix in the remaining ½ tsp turmeric, the red chilli powder, garam masala and salt to taste. Stir the mixture until all the spices are amalgamated, then add 2 medium-sized glasses of hot water to create a sauce. Bring it to a bubble then lower the heat, add the fish, cover and simmer gently for 10 minutes, or until the fish is cooked through. Serve garnished with fresh coriander leaves.

Great with:

Cumin rice.

Keralan coconut fish curry

AJITHA, SENIOR PROGRAMME OFFICER AT ASHA'S HEAD OFFICE

Ajitha comes from Kerala in southern India, and this recipe is typical of food from that region. Fresh fish abounds, as do coconuts, curry leaves and tamarind, giving the curry its distinctive taste. The dish has a vibrant reddy-orange colour, and tastes spicy, tangy and sour all at once. Don't worry about the spice masking the taste of the fish: oily fish carries chilli heat really well. Of course, if you prefer a milder curry, then just reduce the amount of chilli you use, but don't be tempted to reduce the tamarind. It is that which gives the dish its characteristic tang.

SERVES 4

500g fresh oily fish e.g. tuna, snapper or salmon, cleaned and cut into medium-sized chunks
1 snackpot of fresh coconut chunks (or 100g frozen shredded coconut)
10g fresh root ginger, peeled and roughly chopped
2 tsp red chilli powder (Kashmiri if available)
½ tsp ground turmeric
1–2 tbsp tamarind paste
Salt to taste
1 tsp coconut oil
5–6 curry leaves
1 thin green chilli cut into diagonal slices

Optional garnish:

Extra coconut oil
Fresh curry leaves
2 thin green chillies
2 shallots

Lightly sprinkle the fish pieces with salt. Put the fresh coconut in a blender with the ginger and process to create a thick paste. Add a splash of water if necessary to help it come together, but do not make it too runny. Try to get it as smooth as possible, so the resultant sauce does not contain too many bits.

In a bowl, gently mix the fish together with the coconut paste, chilli powder, ground turmeric and tamarind paste. Add up to 3 cups of water and combine well. It should be thin, but not watery, so add the water gradually.

Put the fish mixture into a large pan, add the curry leaves and green chilli slices and cook over a medium heat for 20–30 mins until the fish is cooked through and the curry has thickened slightly. Drizzle with coconut oil and serve hot with rice.

Variation:

For extra authenticity, garnish with 2 thin green chillies slit in half and a few curry leaves fried with the sliced shallots in coconut oil. For a creamier coconut taste, add a small tin (160ml) coconut cream instead of some of the water.

Amritsari fish tikka

AMITAVA, MEMBER OF ASHA COMMUNICATIONS TEAM AT BHIKAJI OFFICE

Amitava made this for us with a boneless, freshwater fish called basa. It is mild in flavour and forks into attractive, soft, white flakes when cooked. Sustainably caught cod, haddock or pollock would all make great alternatives. This deep-fried dish would make a fun, Indian version of fish and chips: maybe consider sweet potato fries, garlic mayo and some coriander chutney on the side to complete the transformation. Otherwise serve with rice, a vegetable dish and chutneys for a more authentic meal.

SERVES 3–4

500g fresh boneless white fish, cut into large-ish chunks
3 tsp ginger-garlic paste (see page 10)
1 tsp mild red chilli powder
¼ tsp ground turmeric
½ tsp carom seeds (or oregano if you don't have them)
½ tbsp plain yoghurt
Salt to taste

For the batter:
50g gram flour
½ tsp ground turmeric
½ tsp salt
1 egg, lightly beaten

Vegetable oil for deep frying

Optional:
Lemon wedges to serve

Dry the fish with kitchen roll and set aside. In a bowl, mix together the ginger-garlic paste with the spices, yoghurt and salt. Combine well then coat the fish with the mixture and leave to one side for 30 minutes.

Make the batter by mixing the gram flour, turmeric and salt in a bowl. Whisk in the egg and 2–3 tablespoons of cold water until you have a smooth, runny batter with the consistency of double cream. Heat the oil in a deep-sided pan or wok, no more than a third full, until really hot, dip the fish pieces in the batter and fry in batches of 4 or 5 pieces, turning once, until they are crispy and golden brown.

Serve immediately with lemon wedges to squeeze over.

Variation:

If you want to avoid frying altogether, this can be converted into a tandoori-style recipe. Increase the yoghurt to 2 tablespoons, omit the batter and add a teaspoon of tandoori paste to the marinade. Coat the fish, leave for 30 minutes then put the pieces on a wire rack over a baking tray in a very hot oven (220°C, fan 200°C, gas mark 7) for 5–10 minutes until cooked through.

paneer

Malai kofta

SONI, SUPERVISOR OF ASHA MOBILE HEALTH CLINICS

Soni seems to love a challenge, both in her personal and professional life. Her eyes sparkled as she recounted to us that thirty-eight years ago, when she was newly married and dining out with her husband in Delhi, she ordered this creamy vegetarian kofta dish. Intrigued by the delicious taste and melting texture which lingered in her mind, she set about re-creating it at home. This is the result, which she has been making ever since, to much acclaim in her family. Do give it a try, it is really amazing. As well as loving cooking, Soni loves her work. She first met Dr Kiran Martin in 1989, within a year of Asha's founding. She says her life's purpose is to serve the poor, and she finds enormous satisfaction in helping permanently transform communities for the better.

SERVES 4

8 slices white bread, crusts cut off
Salt to taste
¼ tsp carom seeds, or oregano if you don't have them
Up to ½ tsp red chilli powder
Leaves from 2–3 stems of fresh coriander, finely chopped, with more to garnish
110g paneer (Indian cheese), mashed (if homemade) otherwise coarsely grated
20–24 sultanas
2 tbsp vegetable oil or ghee
2 small onions, roughly chopped
200g tomatoes, roughly chopped
2 tbsp ginger-garlic paste (see page 10)
¼ tsp ground turmeric
1 tbsp ground coriander
1 tsp garam masala
200ml milk
200ml double cream
Fresh coriander leaves to garnish

Soak each slice of bread in a bowl of water until soft, lift out, squeeze the water out and set the bread aside in a large bowl. Add to the squeezed-out bread the salt, carom seeds, a pinch of red chilli powder and the fresh chopped coriander leaves. Mash the mixture together with your hands to make a soft, pliable texture, like minced meat. Wet your palms, then divide the mixture into eight.

Take each section and flatten into a round patty. Fill it with an eighth of the grated paneer (1½ tsp) and 2–3 sultanas then close into a ball or egg shape. Heat the oil or ghee in a karhai, saute pan or large frying pan over a medium heat and fry the kofta until they are golden all over. (Start with the sealed side to help keep them intact.) Remove with a slotted spoon and set aside.

Puree the onions in a blender or mini chopper (with a splash of water if needed) and set aside. Repeat with the tomatoes. Take the same pan, adding another spoon of oil or ghee if needed, and fry the onion puree with the ginger-garlic paste until golden brown. Mix the spices (turmeric, ¼ teaspoon chilli powder, ground coriander, and garam masala) with a little water to form a thin paste. Add this to the pan with a little salt. Stir until the mixture is fragrant and the oil is separating out, then add the tomatoes. Mix the milk and cream together and add to the pan. Turn the heat down and bring the sauce to the boil. Once it is gently simmering, add in the kofta, cover and cook for 5 minutes. Uncover, then stir constantly but gently until the sauce is a creamy coating consistency. Add a splash of hot water if it gets too thick. Serve sprinkled with fresh coriander leaves.

Gyanwati, Kalkaji

Gyanwati serves us healthy spinach curry, and we sit and ask how her connection with Asha came about. It started in a very hard season, back when her children were little. 'I didn't go out,' she says, 'and I knew nothing.' Without good healthcare, on a basic diet and in a neighbourhood with poor hygiene, the consequences of being uninformed were serious. 'My son became sick,' she says, 'he suffered dehydration and was in hospital for 19 days, but it was too late to rehydrate him and he died.' He was just two years old.

Following this tragedy, Gyanwati was determined to do something positive. 'I never wanted anyone else to go through the same thing,' she explains. Asha staff came to their house and persuaded her husband to let Gyanwati attend classes in basic healthcare. She started coming into the Asha centre and was later trained as a Community Health Volunteer, learning how to keep her home clean and how to prevent and treat common illnesses. She was taught how to make up rehydration fluid and to know when to escalate a case to Asha's medics. She started teaching the same skills to other mothers in Kalkaji slum. Soni, the team leader who showed her what to do, is still working with Asha today. Learning the importance of these simple techniques has saved many lives. Gyanwati is motivated by a powerful connection to those she helps. 'In the 20 years since then,' she says, 'in my community of 400 families, not one child has died of dehydration.'

We marvel at the story we've just heard, told with such modesty. We appreciate this strong woman who has risen above her past. 'I serve in the community centre,' she tells us. 'I'm not here to earn money. I'm fortunate to be part of Asha because if you have hope, everything is easier.'

Her altruism is all the more impressive when she explains that her husband has a spinal injury. He is able to walk now, but was bed-bound for two years. We ask about her husband's opinion of her work in the community. She tells us he is proud of her. People tell him how much she's helped them. 'I have an identity in the community now. I'm the oldest woman in the group, so when they have a problem, they come to me. Everybody knows me.' She has come a long way from knowing nothing and no-one.

Palak paneer

GYANWATI, COMMUNITY HEALTH VOLUNTEER AT KALKAJI SLUM

Palak paneer, or saag paneer as we tend to know it here, is another north Indian staple. For Gyanwati, that means she cooks it about once a month, as she explains that it is costly to make. She saves it as a treat to serve guests or the family on special occasions. Gyanwati is a strong woman who is hugely respected in the community. The iron-rich green of this dish seemed appropriately mirrored in the green edge of her lovely sari. I have modified the chilli level, reducing it from the very spicy version that she cooked us. Of course, if you are feeling adventurous or like a good chilli kick from your food, then double up the chillies. Great with rice or bread and some dal on the side.

SERVES 4

800g spinach, washed and chopped
2 tbsp vegetable oil
¼ tsp cumin seeds
2 medium onions, finely chopped
2 thin green chillies, finely chopped
½ tsp ground coriander
½ tsp ground black pepper
1 clove
Salt to taste
4–6 garlic cloves, finely chopped
2 large tomatoes, cut into small chunks
2 tbsp plain yoghurt
500g paneer (Indian cheese), cut into cubes
Fresh coriander leaves to garnish

Put the prepared spinach into a large pan with a 2–3 tablespoons of boiling water and cook until soft and wilted (5 minutes). Tip into a blender and blitz to form a thick, green puree. Set aside.

Heat the oil in a large frying pan and when it is hot, add the cumin seeds. Let them sizzle for a minute or two, then add the chopped onions and green chillies. Cook, stirring regularly until the onions are golden.

Add all the dry spices, salt and stir well. Once they are fragrant, turn the heat down and add the garlic, tomatoes and yoghurt and cook until the tomatoes are really soft. Add in the cubed paneer and spinach puree, with a splash of water if necessary to keep the sauce moist. Simmer gently for 5 minutes until the paneer is soft and heated through. Garnish with fresh coriander and serve immediately.

Variation:

Gyanwati likes the addition of the yoghurt because it adds a slightly sour tang. Omit this for a more classic treatment, or add a pinch of sugar if you want the creaminess without the acidity.

Muttar paneer

ANANDI, COMMUNITY HEALTH VOLUNTEER AT ZAKHIRA SLUM

Anandi leads us through the dark maze of narrow slum lanes to her home; she is easy to follow in her sunny yellow sari. Unusually, she has an extra room at the front of her home which she uses as a kitchen (many families live in just one room). The ingredients for muttar paneer are all prepped and laid out neatly in small metal bowls: squeaky white cubes of paneer, fresh shelled peas, chopped vegetables and colourful mounds of spices. As she works with an air of quiet confidence, her multi-coloured bangles sparkle in the muted light. This is a classic north Indian dish, which Anandi expertly cooked for us. The sweetness of the peas, the creaminess of the cheese and the gently spiced tomato sauce really are a great combination.

SERVES 3–4

4 tomatoes, cut into chunks

1 medium-large onion, roughly chopped

2 thin green chillies, roughly chopped (optional)

4 large cloves garlic

2 tbsp vegetable oil

250g paneer (Indian cheese), cubed

250g fresh or frozen peas

1 heaped tsp ground coriander

¼ tsp red chilli powder

¼ tsp ground turmeric

¼ tsp garam masala (optional)

Salt to taste

Fresh coriander leaves to garnish

First, put the tomatoes, onion, chillies and garlic cloves in a blender and grind to a smooth paste; set aside.

Heat the oil in a frying pan, and when it is hot, add the paneer. Fry until it is light golden-brown at the edges, stirring it well so that it doesn't burn. Remove with a slotted spoon to a plate topped with a piece of kitchen roll and set aside.

Pour the tomato mixture into the pan, add the peas and cook for another 3–4 minutes. Next, add all the dry spices and salt; stir well. Cook for another 2 minutes then add the cheese back into the sauce. Lower the heat, cover and cook until the paneer is hot and the sauce clings thickly to the cheese and vegetables. Garnish with plenty of fresh coriander and serve immediately.

Variation:

Anandi likes to eat this as a dryish dish, but if you want a wetter, saucier curry, add a small glass of boiling water to the peas when you add the tomato paste. She also explained that some cooks add ¼–½ teaspoons of garam masala with the other dry spices, but her family prefer the flavour without it.

Shahi paneer

RANI, SUPERVISOR OF MANY ASHA SLUM PROJECTS

This dish is creamy, rich and satisfying and one of my favourite things to order when I am in Delhi. Having eaten it everywhere from the YWCA to the old heritage restaurants within the colonnades of Connaught Place, the cheese seems to be rarely cubed – unlike most paneer dishes – but more often cut into delicate slices, triangles or even semi-circles. This reflects the special nature of the dish, that harks back to Mughlai tradition. *Shahi* means 'royal' in Hindi, and this dish is often made with the addition of cashew nuts, saffron and even dried fruit. Rani's version is delicious and nut-free, but I have indicated as a variation where to include cashew nuts if you prefer. Serve with rice or naan.

SERVES 5–6

500g paneer (Indian cheese), sliced into 1cm-thin fingers or triangles
4 tbsp vegetable oil or ghee
1 large onion, finely chopped
6–8 medium tomatoes, finely chopped
1 tsp ginger-garlic paste (see page 10)
1 heaped tsp red chilli powder
½ tsp ground turmeric
2 tbsp ground coriander
¼ tsp dried fenugreek leaves
¼ tsp garam masala, with more to garnish
Salt to taste
125ml single cream, with more to garnish
Fresh coriander leaves to garnish

First, soak your shop-bought paneer to get the lovely softness of homemade Indian paneer: cut it into thin fingers, then soak it in a bowl of boiling water for 5 minutes until soft and springy. Drain well and set aside.

Heat oil or ghee in a karhai, saute pan or medium-sized saucepan. Add the onion and saute lightly until golden brown. Add the tomatoes and cook for 10–12 minutes or until they are pulpy. Transfer the mixture to a blender and blend to a paste with a little water.

Put the same pan back on a medium heat, adding a bit more oil if needed, then add the ginger-garlic paste. Fry for 1–2 minutes then add the chilli powder, turmeric, ground coriander, fenugreek leaves, garam masala and salt. Stir well for a few seconds until the masala mixture is fragrant, then add the tomato-onion paste back into the pan. Cook for 2–3 minutes until the sauce is well blended and heated through. Add a splash of water if needed.

Turn the heat down low and gently fold in the paneer. Cook for 2–3 minutes. Finally swirl in the cream and stir for 1 minute until the sauce is glossy and everything is amalgamated. Garnish with a drizzle of cream, fresh coriander and a sprinkling of garam masala and serve immediately.

Variation:

Add 15–20 cashew nuts with the onions and continue with the paste as above for a thicker, creamier sauce. You could also infuse the cream with a generous pinch of saffron for 10 minutes on a low heat, before adding it as above.

vegetables

Thoran

Rama has been a nurse at the Asha polyclinic in Ekta Vihar for the last 12 years. She demonstrated this southern Indian vegetable dish to us on her way to run an outpatients clinic. She explained that she chose this recipe as it is healthy and easy to cook. A *thoran* is a stir-fried 'dry' vegetable dish containing fresh coconut. If you have never had one before, do try it. It is quite unlike the richly spiced Indian vegetable dishes we are used to, being fresher, crunchier and more vibrant. I'd suggest prepping all the veg before you start cooking, as once it is underway, it doesn't take long.

SERVES 4

2–3 tbsp vegetable oil or
  coconut oil
¼ tsp black mustard seeds
1 tsp urad dal (if you have it)
2 dried red chillies
1 small onion, very finely sliced
1 thin green chilli, very finely
  chopped
Salt to taste
¼ tsp ground turmeric
100g white cabbage, very finely
  shredded
1 large or 2 small carrots,
  coarsely grated
150g green beans, finely
  chopped
12–15 curry leaves, roughly
  chopped
3 heaped tbsp grated coconut,
  fresh or frozen

Heat the oil in a karhai, wok or large frying pan over a high heat until it is hot. Add the mustard seeds, urad dal and dried red chillies and fry for 2 minutes until the mustard seeds start popping. Add the sliced onions, green chilli and stir fry for another 2 minutes until they soften. Sprinkle in the salt and turmeric and mix to combine.

Tip in the cabbage, carrots, green beans, curry leaves and coconut and stir fry for 5–7 minutes until the vegetables are just tender. Add a splash of water if needed to stop anything sticking to the pan. Serve immediately, on its own, as a side dish or with some yoghurt and lime pickle.

Rajwati, Savda Ghevra

We have driven 18 miles from New Delhi, past factories and scrubland. In the haze we see people walking in the fields. Soon we turn into a broad, concrete street and pass low-rise houses, where children are playing cricket with a makeshift polystyrene bat. We kick off our shoes at Rajwati's door and enter her home. She is the area's Community Health Volunteer and is a gifted leader who also assumes many of the duties of an Asha Team Leader. With a smile she welcomes us and eagerly shows us to the back of her home, where we find a roomful of women sitting together. We spend the morning learning how to make their food.

This area, Savda, is not a slum as such because residents own their own land. It was not always like this: they used to live in a district of Delhi called Thokar Number Eight.

Slumlords often turn a blind eye to people living on their land, until they want the land back. In 2010, New Delhi hosted the Commonwealth Games and the government needed to build a flyover. The residents of Thokar No. 8 Slum were only given a few hours' notice to leave, despite assurances given to Asha that the community was not under threat. That evening, bulldozers demolished their homes. People fled and spent the night under whatever shelter they could make for themselves, many at the roadside. Days turned into weeks.

In the hours after it first happened, Dr Kiran met with the people and immediately got to work to ensure justice for those displaced. The government agreed to an immediate distribution of food and water and in time made a survey of need. Dr Kiran had to knock on many ministers' doors, including the chief minister of Delhi, to get the work done. Dr Kiran's determination and persistence yielded fruit: after three months a resettlement was agreed. The government gave each former household the right to buy land and build a home in a new community they called Savda. There were still challenges to overcome: the land was in a bad state and few of the slum's former residents had the necessary

7,000 rupees to take up the government's offer. Asha worked with government to create loans that the residents could – and did – repay over time. It meant that some of Delhi's poorest people accessed financial services for the first time. This project has grown far beyond its birthplace and has become Asha's Financial Inclusion Programme.

The residents of Savda are landowners and proud of the homes they built, even if infrastructure is still developing. Without mains water, tankers still deliver daily, but 'Water ATMs' have been installed so that if people are at work they can collect their water at a time that suits them, for a small charge.

I ask the women assembled in Rajwati's house which of them were part of the original community in Thokar No. 8. Rajwati says, 'All of us were. We have remained neighbours.' One of them stands up and stretches out an arm to show me. She moves around and lightly touches the top of her friends' heads, with a grace that makes it look like a blessing.

Aloo saag

RAJWATI, COMMUNITY HEALTH VOLUNTEER AT SAVDA GHEVRA

Rajwati loves to feed people and her reputation preceded her: we were told to skip breakfast the day we were visiting her home. Rajwati had organised a large number of dishes to be prepared for us. We sat meeting her friends, gradually tasting their food, and as we chatted she would pop extra mouthfuls into our mouths if we weren't deemed to be eating enough. Rajwati made a lasting impression on me, not only for her strength of character and generous hospitality, but also for her culinary skills. This simple potato dish was the most memorable thing I ate that day: delicious fried crescents of golden potato coated with garlic and chilli-infused greens. She used fresh fenugreek leaves (*methi*) and rehydrates dried ones when they are not in season. They have a unique, bitter taste but by all means use baby spinach instead.

SERVES 3–4 as a side dish

2–3 tbsp vegetable oil
2 cloves garlic, finely chopped
1–2 dried red chillies, broken in half
Pinch asafoetida (if you have it)
500g potatoes, peeled and chopped into cubes or small wedges
Salt to taste
250g fresh fenugreek, leaves only, or baby spinach, very finely shredded

Heat the oil in a karhai or lidded frying pan over a very low heat and when it is warm add the garlic, red chilli and asafoetida. Let them gently infuse their flavour into the oil for 5–10 minutes, ensuring the garlic doesn't brown.

Add the prepared potatoes and fry them over a medium-low heat for 10 minutes. Add salt to taste and the chopped leaves. Stir to mix everything together, cover and cook for another 10–15 minutes until the potatoes are completely tender. Serve hot.

Spiced butternut squash

MONIKA, STAFF MEMBER AT KALKAJI SLUM

Monika cooks every day with her father. They plan the family menu on a daily basis; he cooks the 'non-veg' dishes, and she cooks the vegetable dishes as she is a vegetarian. This delicious dish features in summer when pumpkins are plentiful in India, and is a popular choice at weddings and festivals. She recommends eating it hot or cold with fresh pooris and green coriander chutney. Here we have used butternut squash instead, which we have the luxury of getting all year round, but any squash or pumpkin would work just as well.

SERVES 4–5

4–5 tbsp vegetable oil

2–3 bay leaves

½ tsp cumin seeds

¼ tsp black peppercorns (or lots of freshly ground black pepper)

1 cinnamon stick (up to 10cm)

¼ tsp asafoetida (if you have it)

2 medium onions, finely chopped

1 tbsp ginger-garlic paste (see page 10)

1 butternut squash, peeled and chopped into cubes

2 large or 3 small tomatoes, finely chopped

1 tsp red chilli powder

1 tsp ground turmeric

1 tsp ground coriander

Salt to taste

½ tsp garam masala

Fresh coriander to garnish

Heat the oil in a karhai, wok or large saute pan with a lid and when it is hot, add the bay leaves, cumin seeds, peppercorns, cinnamon stick and asafoetida and fry in the hot oil until aromatic (1–2 minutes).

Add the chopped onions and ginger-garlic paste and fry over a medium heat, stirring well until the onions are light brown on the edges. Add the chopped butternut squash and tomatoes, mix well, cover and cook for a few minutes.

Remove the lid, add the chilli powder, turmeric, ground coriander and salt and stir well. Cover again and cook for another 10 minutes or until the butternut squash is tender, adding a splash of water to prevent it sticking if necessary.

Uncover, stir well and sprinkle with garam masala and fresh coriander. Serve hot or cold.

Great with:

Pooris and chutney.

Aloo tamater curry

ANGURI, MEMBER OF WOMEN'S GROUP AT JEEWAN NAGAR SLUM

Anguri has lived in Jeewan Nagar slum for 25 years, for the last ten of which she has been a member of the women's group. Her eyes shine as she says how loved and supported she feels. After Anguri's husband died last year, Asha team leader Kulwinder helped her claim her widow's pension, for which she is immensely grateful. She now lives with her daughter, son, daughter-in-law and grandchild, so she still has many mouths to feed. This potato and tomato curry is wholesome, tasty and one of her everyday favourites, which she serves with fresh chapattis or pooris. Use plump, ripe tomatoes for the best flavour and colour.

SERVES 3–4

2 large (baking size) potatoes, peeled, diced or thinly sliced
2–3 tbsp vegetable oil
½ tsp cumin seeds
1 bay leaf
1 medium onion, chopped
1 thin green chilli, very finely chopped (optional)
¼ tsp garam masala
¼ tsp red chilli powder
¼ tsp ground coriander
¼ tsp ground turmeric
3 large tomatoes, roughly chopped
Salt to taste
Fresh coriander to garnish

Put the chopped potatoes into a pan, cover with boiling water, add a good pinch of salt and cook until just tender. Drain and set aside.

Heat the oil in a karhai or saucepan over a high heat until it is hot. Add the cumin seeds and bay leaf, let them sizzle for a moment or two, then add the chopped onion and green chilli and cook until the onion is tinged brown at the edges (6–7 minutes). Add all the powdered spices and let them cook for a few minutes to develop a good masala base for the dish. Add the chopped tomatoes, stir well until they soften, then add salt to taste and turn the heat down. Cook for 5 minutes to let the flavours mingle and develop.

Add the cooked potatoes to the pan with a small glass of water to create a sauce. Stir gently, cover, and simmer for 10 minutes until everything is really soft and the sauce is not too thin. Serve hot garnished with fresh coriander.

Variation:
Add some frozen peas at the end if you want an even more veg-rich main course.

Rabiya, Mayapuri

Rabiya's clothes catch my eye as we arrive at Mayapuri because of their understated, rich colours: an iridescent mixture of burgundy and black. She doesn't push herself forward, so it is only later, when she brings us her food and tells us her story, that we see her lovely smile, along with her strength.

'Who is the main cook in your family?' we ask. (We've met several women her age who share duties with their mothers or take it all on themselves).
'I cook for my three daughters and my husband.'
'How old are your daughters?'
'They are in class 4, class 2 and in nursery.'
We check our notes: she is just 23. She had her eldest when she was 13.

'I don't want my daughters to make the same mistakes I made,' she says, which is poignant, coming from such a young woman. When Rabiya describes what happened, I muse that, far from having made mistakes, she had handled with great maturity circumstances she had not chosen. She had made a good life for her family, with a great life still ahead of her.

Her father had been unemployed. Needing fewer mouths to feed, they had Rabiya married off, allowing her upkeep to be her husband's worry: needs must. At that time Rabiya was still in school, so her education came to an abrupt end, age 13, when she started married life. Days filled with keeping house, cooking and caring for her husband. Soon she was caring for children too, at an age when most of her peers were just learning how to roll chapattis.

She knew no-one when she moved to Mayapuri, having grown up elsewhere in Delhi. Asha's women's group provided an easy place to come and talk to other women and start to make local friends. She has been a member for ten years.

Rabiya never learnt to cook with her mother so the only dishes she could make at first were dal

and rice. After marriage she started experimenting with food, and enjoyed it. 'It's a way to be creative,' she ventured. She swishes her scarf back over her shoulder with slender fingers. 'If I get a new recipe I get excited. If someone in the area is cooking for a party, I help them out.' She serves us her potatoes and peas with cauliflower (*aloo muttar gobi*) which is delicious, and uses seasonal, winter vegetables. Vegetable stalls here only sell seasonal produce, so people really enjoy their favourites when their season returns. She talks us through her recipe clearly and adds details that reveal her skills both as a versatile cook and a good teacher.

Amanda asks, 'Have you ever thought about teaching others to cook?' She nods, 'I thought about it, but I have little children. Maybe in a few years that will be possible.' We ask her what her husband thinks. Her face lights up: 'He is supportive of everything I do.'

Aloo muttar gobi

RABIYA, MEMBER OF WOMEN'S GROUP AT MAYAPURI SLUM

Rabiya loves to cook and she smiled happily as she said she makes this dish two to three times a week for her young family. It is a winter favourite, made when cauliflowers are in season and are firm and plump. She makes this as a 'dry' vegetable dish. However, she said if you want more sauce – to eat it as a curry – you should slightly increase the amount of spices and then pour in two small cups of water. As a mother of three young girls, it seemed unsurprising that she served her delicious vegetable medley in pretty pink fluted dishes: just what her daughters would love.

SERVES 4–6 as a side dish

3–4 tbsp vegetable oil
1 small cauliflower, cut into very
    small florets
2 medium-sized potatoes,
    peeled and cubed
2 tsp ginger-garlic paste (see
    page 10)
¼ tsp ground cumin
¼ tsp ground coriander
¼ tsp ground turmeric
¼ tsp red chilli powder
¼ tsp fenugreek seeds
2 medium tomatoes, very finely
    chopped
Salt to taste
250g frozen peas
Fresh coriander to garnish

Heat two tablespoons of the oil in a karhai or frying pan over a high heat. Add the cauliflower and stir fry until golden. Remove with a slotted spoon and set aside. Add the potatoes and fry until they are also golden brown all over. Remove to join the cauliflower and set aside.

If needed, add another tablespoon or two of oil and heat until hot. Add the ginger-garlic paste, fry for a minute then add all the dry spices and the fenugreek seeds. Stir for a moment, then tip in the chopped tomatoes; stir well until they soften and add salt to taste.

Add the cooked potato and cauliflower back into the pan and mix everything together. Add the frozen peas and a few spoonfuls of water, so the mixture is wet but there is not a sauce as such. Cover and simmer until the peas are cooked and the potatoes are just tender. Be careful not to overcook the vegetables. Serve hot, garnished with fresh coriander.

Aloo beans

HEMLATA, TEAM LEADER AT KANAK DURGA

Hemlata has a lovely open face, unlined by worry or age, and a wide, happy smile. She has been team leader at the Asha centre in Kanak Durga slum for a year. She smiles modestly as she says how proud she feels to be the youngest team leader of an Asha slum project. She explains how much she has learnt from supervisors like Rani and Soni, and how she readily seeks Rani's counsel if she needs it. She likes the bonds that come from overseeing the women's group, youth group and children's group and the sense of family they create in the community. She cooks this dish about once a week, as beans and potatoes are available in Delhi all year round. It is quick, easy and great eaten with chapattis as either a main course or as a side dish. If you like your beans a little more *al dente*, reduce the cooking time accordingly.

SERVES 4–6 as a side dish

3–4 tbsp vegetable oil
½ tsp cumin seeds
350g potatoes, peeled and cubed
¼ tsp ground turmeric
500g green beans, washed and sliced into 1–2cm lengths
Salt to taste
½ tsp ground black pepper
½ tsp red chilli powder
½ tsp ground coriander
Fresh coriander to garnish

Heat the oil in a karhai, wok or large frying pan over a high heat until it is hot. Add the cumin seeds and fry for a minute until they sizzle. Add the potatoes and turmeric and mix to combine. Fry for a couple of minutes.

Add the green beans and salt. Cover the pan, letting the vegetables cook for 8–10 minutes on a low heat. Add the black pepper, red chilli and ground coriander and mix well to coat the vegetables in the spices. Fry, stirring regularly, for 5–10 minutes until the vegetables are tender. Sprinkle with fresh chopped coriander and serve immediately.

Baingan bharta

HASEENA, COMMUNITY HEALTH VOLUNTEER AT TRILOKPURI SLUM

Haseena wears a beautiful and appropriately purple patterned scarf as she demonstrates this classic aubergine dish. She explains that she used to roast the aubergine directly over a flame – the traditional method to give a smoky flavour – but now fries it instead for simplicity. Her new method is outlined below, with the alternative listed as a variation. Do whichever appeals: either way you want the aubergine to have a completely soft, creamy texture. This is delicious scooped onto hot, puffy naan, served as a dip or to accompany lamb.

SERVES 4 as a side dish

1 medium aubergine
3–4 tbsp vegetable oil
Salt to taste
½ tsp cumin seeds
2 small red onions, finely
   chopped
1 thin green chilli, very finely
   chopped (optional)
2 cloves garlic, finely chopped
   or minced
1 large tomato, finely chopped
Fresh coriander to garnish

Peel the aubergine, cut into small cubes and fry in a hot pan with 2 tablespoons of the oil on a medium heat. Add a pinch of salt, stir well, cover and lower the heat. Cook for 10 minutes until it is completely soft. Tip onto a plate and mash coarsely. Set aside.

Heat the remaining oil in a karhai or frying pan over a high heat until it is hot. Add the cumin seeds and when they are sizzling, add the chopped onion and green chilli and cook until the onion is tinged brown at the edges. Add the garlic, cook for a minute or two, then tip in the chopped tomato, stirring until it softens and disintegrates. Add the mashed aubergine, check for salt and turn the heat down. Cook for 10 minutes to let the flavours develop, adding a splash of water if it looks a bit dry. Serve hot garnished with fresh coriander.

Variation:

For a smokier flavour, put the aubergine directly over a medium gas flame and cook for 7–8 minutes, turning it with tongs, until the skin is blistered and blackened. Leave to cool, then peel off the skin and mash as before. Alternatively, cook on the barbecue or under a very hot grill until charred. You can add a teaspoon of ground coriander with the garlic, and sprinkle in a half teaspoon of garam masala at the end if you want.

Spinach with tomatoes and ginger

KULWINDER, TEAM LEADER AT JEEWAN NAGAR SLUM

Kulwinder cooked us a favourite seasonal Punjabi dish called *sarson ka saag* (mustard greens). Her version was made with equal quantities of mustard leaves and spinach, with some fenugreek leaves for added tang; some recipes use all mustard leaves. It is an eagerly anticipated winter speciality eaten with *maki ki roti* (corn flatbreads) and butter. Whilst few people in the UK will easily find the three leaves to make her authentic version, you can use spinach alone, especially baby spinach, to make the dish quicker to cook, and still very appealing. I loved the iron-rich, dark green leaves married with tomatoes, ginger and spice. Kulwinder cooks big batches of the leaves when they are in season and keeps them in the fridge, ready to fry a portion each time she makes the finished dish.

SERVES 4

500g baby spinach, washed and chopped into 1cm strips

2–3 tbsp vegetable oil

2 small onions, finely chopped

2 small green chillies, very finely chopped

5–6 cm root ginger, peeled and finely chopped or grated

4 cloves garlic, finely chopped

2 medium tomatoes, roughly chopped

1 tsp garam masala

Salt to taste

20g cornmeal

20g unsalted butter

Put the chopped spinach into a large pan and cover with boiling water. Cook until the leaves have wilted and stalks are soft (2–3 minutes). Drain well.

Heat the oil in a karhai or pan over a high heat until it is hot. Add the chopped onion and green chilli and cook until the onion is tinged brown at the edges. Add the ginger and garlic and cook for a few minutes, stirring regularly. Tip in the chopped tomato, garam masala, salt and cornmeal and stir well. Once the tomato has softened, add the spinach back into the pan with half a small glass of water. Mix well, add salt and butter, turn the heat down and simmer uncovered for 5–10 minutes until the mixture is soft and has thickened, but is still a lovely vivid green.

Serve hot with corn bread or chapattis and extra butter.

Variation:

If you like a smoother texture, liquidise the spinach with a splash of its cooking water.

Rajendri, Trilokpuri

Rajendri sits on the floor chatting to us as her *aloo gobi* cooks. We are discovering many differences between her life and our own. For her family's meals she follows a routine: vegetables with rice one day; dal with rice the next. They eat chicken once a week. This pattern seems widespread in the slums. Children here look healthy but many are short for their age compared to their counterparts in the UK.

Vendors' carts and blankets at the roadside are piled high with good quality, nutritious seasonal produce. Only seasonal produce is available in the slums, except for onions and tomatoes, which are available all year round. However, vegetables are too expensive for the very poorest: they manage with watered-down dal with rice. Pickles are a popular addition to meals because they provide tastes and nutrients out of season, using produce bought in season, when prices are relatively low. Refrigeration is rare, so pickles are popular and often homemade. Fruit and vegetables are pickled whole or sliced: Rajendri's favourite is mango. Chutneys here are fresh, often herby mixtures that add colour, variety and nutrition to the meal.

Through her involvement with Asha, Rajendri says she has discovered many good things. She joined the women's group five years ago, after coming for medications for her children. She loves how they eat together, gossip together, even go places together. Unusually for women in her culture, the women now go on picnics in a nearby park.

Her bonds with the other women are not just social. She has fought battles with government alongside these women, such as the time when they convinced the authorities to supply water to their community. Basic infrastructure that we take for granted can be non-existent in slums unless people like Rajendri lobby local officials, with support from Asha.

Now an Asha Community Health Volunteer (CHV), Rajendri is responsible for 200 households, visiting ten of them each day. She gives advice, simple treatments and is trained to recognise symptoms of certain illnesses. 'I have a routine. If someone is unwell, but not needing hospital, I find time the next day to visit them again, or I might tell the other CHVs that a visit was needed and ask them to update me.' Asha has excellent facilities for medical testing, treatment and making referrals elsewhere. I'm impressed that the burden of care is well spread across the community.

Rajendri has a peaceful way about her and she is not burdened by her community's needs. As she talks, it is clear that she enjoys her work. 'Every decision is taken together. If there is a major disturbance in the community, we can now go to the police. I can explain things to my family about health and saving money. In the past, my husband wouldn't allow me to go out, but now he sees the changes for good and he is happy too.'

Aloo gobi

RAJENDRI, COMMUNITY HEALTH VOLUNTEER AT TRILOKPURI SLUM

Rajendri squats comfortably, her pink and white *salwar kameez* gathered neatly around her, as she demonstrates this classic potato and cauliflower combination. Popular in the UK and in northern India, this is a delicious and simple vegetable dish. Rajendri stir fries the cauliflower and potatoes separately before combining them with the other ingredients. This results in a fresh-tasting, vibrant texture and flavour, quite unlike some of the soggy versions we may be more familiar with from our local curry house. It is now a firm favourite when I want a 'dry' vegetable side dish.

SERVES 4 as a side dish

4–5 tbsp vegetable oil
½ cauliflower, cut into very small florets
2 large baking potatoes, peeled and diced
1 small onion, chopped
2–3 thin green chillies, very finely chopped (optional)
1 tsp ginger-garlic paste (see page 10)
2 medium or large tomatoes, roughly chopped
½ tsp garam masala
¼ tsp ground turmeric
Salt to taste
Fresh coriander to garnish

Heat the oil in a karhai or frying pan over a high heat until it is hot. Add the cauliflower and stir fry until golden. Remove with a slotted spoon and set aside. Add the potatoes and fry until they are also golden brown all over. Remove to join the cauliflower and set aside.

Add the onion and green chillies and cook until the onion is tinged light brown at the edges. Add the ginger-garlic paste, fry for a minute then tip in the chopped tomatoes, stir well until they soften, then add the garam masala and turmeric; salt to taste. Stir well to let the flavours mingle.

Add the cooked potato and cauliflower back into the pan and mix everything together. Add a tiny splash of water if the mixture looks like it is catching on the bottom of the pan, but not too much, as this is a dry dish. Serve hot garnished with fresh coriander.

pulses & rice

Tarka dal

NEERU, HOUSEKEEPER AT ASHA'S BHIKAJI OFFICE

Victoria and I arrived at Asha's Bhikaji office in the early afternoon, tired and hungry from the overnight flight from London, but full of expectation for what lay ahead. Neeru had some red lentils soaking, ready to cook this fresh for us once we had met everyone. We watched attentively over her shoulder as she put this together – something she could have expertly done with her eyes shut – and it was perfect. With a bowl of fluffy basmati rice, some of Shabnam's walnut chutney, and a cup of steaming, gingery chai, it was a simple but memorable late lunch and a fantastic start to our cookbook research!

SERVES 4

200g red lentils (*masoor dal*)
2–3 tbsp vegetable oil
1 tsp cumin seeds
2 small dried red chillies (use fresh green ones if these are not available)
1 medium onion, chopped
1 medium tomato, chopped
½ tsp red chilli powder
1 tsp ground turmeric
¾ tsp ground coriander
Salt to taste
Fresh coriander to garnish

Rinse the lentils in water until it runs clear. Put the lentils in double their volume of water (about 500ml) in a pan and soak for 20 minutes. Then bring to the boil, reduce the heat and simmer for 20 minutes until the lentils become soft and mushy. Add a splash more water if it looks very thick or solid.

Meanwhile, heat the oil in another pan over a high heat until it is really hot. Add the cumin seeds and dried red chillies and fry for a moment until they colour and start to sizzle. Add the chopped onion and cook until it is tinged brown at the edges, then add the chopped tomato and stir well. Once it starts to bubble and soften in the heat (2–3 minutes), add the red chilli powder, turmeric and ground coriander and stir well. Season generously.

Keep cooking until the mixture is uniform and the spices have been cooked through, then add the cooked lentils and their liquid. Mix well and warm through over a gentle heat. Taste to see if any more salt is needed. Serve hot, garnished with fresh coriander.

Variation:

There are many variations of tarka dal, so feel free to experiment and customise this to your taste. I like to add a couple of finely chopped garlic cloves and some fresh curry leaves to mine if I have them to hand. A sprinkling of garam masala is also a nice additional garnish. Part of the charm of this recipe is its simplicity and flexibility – dress it up or down depending on its role in the meal, as star of the show or as a simple, nutritious side dish.

Dal with squash and spinach

KAMLA, COMMUNITY HEALTH VOLUNTEER AT ANNA NAGAR SLUM

Kamla explained that she has a large repertoire of dal recipes that she regularly cooks as they are a mainstay of her family meals. Alongside arhar dal and mung dal, this is one of her favourites, which she made for us with bottle gourd (*lauki*). Understanding that we might not be able to get that, she said we could use any squash or pumpkin instead, or even add spinach. Use whichever you prefer: we have used butternut squash and spinach for extra colour and flavour.

SERVES 3–4

2 tbsp vegetable oil
1 medium onion, sliced into crescents
1–2 thin green chillies, very finely chopped
½ tsp ground turmeric
1 tsp ginger-garlic paste (see page 10)
¼ tsp red chilli powder
1 large tomato, finely chopped
Salt to taste
200g chana dal, soaked in water for an hour and then washed and drained
250g butternut squash, peeled and diced into small cubes or matchsticks
2–3 handfuls baby spinach
Fresh coriander leaves to garnish

Heat the oil in a large karhai or saucepan over a medium-high heat. Add the onion and green chilli and fry until the onion is brown at the edges. Add the turmeric, ginger-garlic paste and chilli powder and stir well, cooking the mixture for 1–2 minutes. Add ½ cup water and turn the heat up until it boils. Add the tomato and cook until it softens and reduces (2–3 minutes).

Add salt, chana dal, butternut squash and 500–600ml of water and simmer for 20–30 minutes, until both the lentils and butternut squash are tender. Taste for seasoning and fold through the baby spinach. When it is wilted, garnish with fresh coriander and serve immediately.

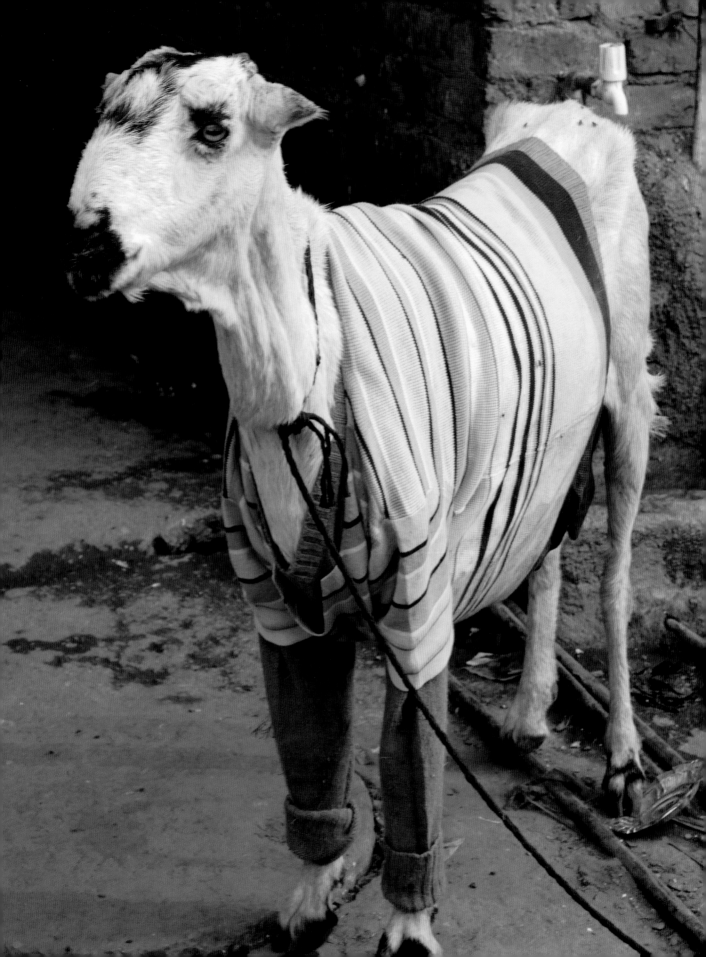

Sanjana, Jeewan Nagar

We are in Jeewan Nagar slum, heading to the home of Sanjana. She is the very effective and well-loved president of her women's group. Turning a corner we find a calm, tucked-away area. The morning light plays artistically on the colourfully painted walls, but in the dark, without our guide, this walk would be difficult and scary.

Soon we are led into a small, neatly organised room where Sanjana lives with her husband and two daughters. She has a calm, modest way about her, so it's only as we ply her with questions that we discover what a powerhouse she is.

Sanjana moved to this slum from the Punjab with her husband back in 2008, two years after Asha started its work in the district. She saw neighbours going to the women's group and followed them there. She discovered it was a place where she could have some respite from her problems, but soon she was working with the other women in the group

to solve problems that were affecting the whole community. She loves serving with Asha because it means she can 'pay it forward' and give someone else the kind of help she received. She has now been president of the women's group for four years.

She educates householders about cleanliness – vital when a community has to provide most of its own sanitation and healthcare – and she works to empower them to send their children to school. In this she has been trained, supported and encouraged by Asha staff, to whom she can escalate any medical needs and bigger issues.

Under the strip light, it's impressive to see her handle the gas stove while wearing a beautiful thin scarf. The royal-blue chiffon has little sequinned swirls of red and gold, which match her glass bangles. Her black hair is swept into a clip. We discover that scarves like these are her husband's work: he is an entrepreneur who started a factory which dyes and finishes clothes. Asha was instrumental in its early days. Sanjana hands us the bowls of mushroom-coloured dal makhani and we tuck into the creamy comfort food. She loves cooking and she laughs with us when she says her husband won't eat anyone else's.

Asha team leader Kulwinder is with us. She smiles as she listens to the stories of past campaigns and she tells us how much she loves Sanjana. Recently they lobbied to have the local police investigate a serious crime that had languished for a month: they responded and just a week later the case was resolved.

Sanjana recalls what it used to be like here a few years ago. The streets of Jeewan Nagar were unlit, so it was a dangerous place to walk after dark. A slum, by definition, is not an official housing development and lies outside the scope of the city planners, but they campaigned, and now the authorities have installed street lighting. 'My youngest daughter is 5 years old,' she says, 'but because of me, she's not afraid of anyone.'

Dal makhani

SANJANA, PRESIDENT OF THE WOMEN'S GROUP, JEEWAN NAGAR SLUM

Dal makhani is a north Indian 'black dal' made with dark urad beans. *Makhan* means 'butter' and this dish is typically cooked with ghee and enriched with cream to complement the beans softened after their long, slow cooking. Unusually, Sanjana adds grated paneer to her delicious version. The end result is rich, earthy, creamy and very moreish.

SERVES 4

150g urad dal (whole black lentils), soaked in water overnight then washed and drained

4 medium tomatoes, roughly chopped

2–3 thin green chillies, roughly chopped

20g ginger-garlic paste (see page 10)

¼ tsp ground turmeric

¼ tsp ground coriander

¼ tsp red chilli powder

3 tbsp ghee or vegetable oil

1 tsp cumin seeds

Pinch of asafoetida (if you have it)

Salt to taste

30g paneer (Indian cheese), finely grated

2 tbsp double cream

Fresh coriander leaves to garnish

Put the pre-soaked urad dal in a large pan of water, so they are covered by 2–3 cm and bring to the boil. Remove any scum that comes to the surface with a spoon. Simmer, covered or semi covered, for 40–60 minutes until they are very soft; set aside. Add a splash more water if necessary to keep the beans covered in water as they cook. In a blender or mini chopper, grind the tomatoes and fresh green chillies together to a coarse paste, and set aside.

Put the ginger-garlic paste in a bowl with the turmeric, ground coriander and chilli powder. Add a little water to make a thin paste. Heat the ghee or oil in another smaller pan over a medium-high heat. Add the cumin seeds and fry for a moment until they colour and start to sizzle, then add the spice paste and cook for 1–2 minutes. Tip in the tomato chilli paste and stir well. Once it starts to bubble, add the asafoetida and salt to taste. Stir in the grated paneer and cook the sauce for another 2–3 minutes.

Tip this mixture into the cooked dal and mix well over a gentle heat. Taste for salt, drizzle over the cream and serve hot, garnished with fresh coriander.

Chana masala

SWEETA, ASHA SUPERVISOR IN MULTIPLE SLUMS

As we tried this tasty dish huddled together with other women in a tiny home, Sweeta explained that this Punjabi speciality is traditionally made with black chickpeas (*kala chana*). Like their paler counterparts, these are prized for being very nutritious: as well as their nutty chickpea taste and buttery texture, they have a high fibre content and are rich in iron. Use whichever you can get hold of. When Sweeta cooks this she uses dried chickpeas, which she soaks overnight and then boils in a pressure cooker. For ease and speed, we have used the tinned version here, making it a quick store cupboard recipe. Sweeta recommends serving this alongside a meat dish, fresh soft chapattis and a creamy mint and garlic raita.

SERVES 4 as a side dish

1 tbsp vegetable oil
½ tsp cumin seeds
2 onions, finely chopped
1 tsp ginger-garlic paste (see page 10)
2–4 thin green chillies, very finely chopped
¼ tsp red chilli powder
½ tsp ground turmeric
1 large tomato, chopped
1 x 400g can chickpeas, drained
Salt to taste
½ bunch fresh coriander, roughly chopped

Heat the oil in a karhai or large saute pan; when it is hot, add the cumin seeds and toss in the hot oil until aromatic (1–2 minutes).

Add the chopped onions and when they start to turn golden at the edges, add the ginger-garlic paste. Fry for 30 seconds then add the chopped green chillies, red chilli powder, turmeric and chopped tomato. Cook over a medium heat for around 3 minutes to create a fragrant masala mixture.

Tip in the drained chickpeas, add a small glass of water and mix well to create a sauce. Cook gently, with the lid on, for 5–10 minutes and add salt to taste. You are not aiming for a very runny curry. Uncover, stir well and fold through plenty of fresh coriander.

Rajma

NEELAM, COMMUNITY HEALTH VOLUNTEER AT PEERA GARHI SLUM

Rajma, or kidney bean curry, is the Indian version of what we might call vegetarian chilli. Made with kidney beans, onions, tomatoes and spices, it is wholesome, nourishing and simple to put together. Perfect as a vegetarian main course or when you have a crowd to feed, it goes brilliantly with breads or rice and is lovely with some creamy raita and coriander chutney on the side. Neelam's version uses fresh tomatoes, but feel free to use tinned plum tomatoes instead. If so, add a teaspoon of sugar.

SERVES 4

250g dried kidney beans, soaked in water overnight and then washed and drained
(or 3 x 400g cans of drained pre-cooked kidney beans)
2 medium onions, roughly chopped
5cm root ginger, peeled
6–8 garlic cloves, peeled
2 tbsp vegetable oil
½ tsp ground turmeric
¾ tsp ground coriander
1 tsp red chilli powder
1 tsp ground cumin
1 tsp garam masala
3–4 large tomatoes or 1 x tin of plum tomatoes
Salt to taste
Fresh coriander leaves to garnish

Put the pre-soaked kidney beans in a large pan of water, so they are covered by 2–3 cm. Bring to the boil and boil for at least 15 minutes (so they are safe to eat) then lower the heat and simmer for 40–60 minutes or until tender, adding more hot water if necessary to keep the beans covered. Set aside.

Blitz the onions, ginger and garlic together in a blender or mini chopper to make a thick paste. Heat the oil in a large karhai or saucepan over a medium-high heat. Add the paste and cook for 10–15 minutes until it turns darker and really fragrant, stirring and adding a splash of water as needed to avoid burning. Add the spices, stir and cook for a couple more minutes. In a blender or mini chopper, grind the tomatoes to a coarse paste and tip this in, along with the kidney beans and a small glass of the cooking liquid or water. Mix well. Add salt to taste, bring to the boil and simmer for 10–15 minutes, adding some more liquid if it gets too dry. Taste for seasoning and serve hot, garnished with plenty of fresh coriander.

Variation:

For a speedier version, use 3 x 400g cans of drained pre-cooked kidney beans.

Cumin rice

SHALINI, TEAM LEADER AT EKTA VIHAR SLUM

Shalini explained to us that there are lots of different grades of rice in India. She prefers using long, thin basmati rice, as she feels the grains are tastier. Apparently basmati gets better with age and the best quality rice is aged for one to two years, which both matures the flavour and results in fluffier more separate grains once cooked. This simple dish elevates ordinary rice up a notch, and is still very quick and easy to do.

SERVES 4

250g basmati rice
2 tbsp ghee or vegetable oil
½ tsp cumin seeds
Salt to taste

Measure the dry rice in a jug and note the volume (as you will need double this volume of water later). Wash the rice in a sieve under cold water, until the water runs clear, then drain.

Put a large pan (that has a well-fitting lid) on the heat, and add the ghee or oil. When it is hot, add the cumin seeds and fry for a minute or two until they are fragrant. Tip in the drained rice and stir well to coat the grains until they are shiny. Add the appropriate quantity of water (double the rice by volume) and salt, stir gently and bring to the boil. Cover with a lid, turn the heat down to low and cook for 8–10 minutes. Turn the heat off, but leave it covered for another 3–4 minutes. Remove the lid, fluff it up with a fork and serve immediately.

Variation:

This is also good garnished with thinly sliced fried onions. Cook them in the pan first, then remove with a slotted spoon before you add the cumin seeds. Mix them into the rice on serving.

Tomato rice

SUMATI, MEMBER OF WOMEN'S GROUP, AT KUSUMPUR SLUM

Sumati explained that this is a typical southern Indian rice dish that she often makes with leftover rice from the night before. However, I think this is also well worth making from scratch. It is absolutely delicious, combining the warm flavours of tomato and garlic enriched with subtle spices and curry leaves. Sumati enjoys this with mango pickle but it would be great with lots of other things, such as Keralan fried fish, one of the coconut chicken dishes or even plain grilled chicken. This is versatile, tasty and also looks absolutely beautiful.

SERVES 2 as a side dish

3 tbsp coconut or vegetable oil
½ tsp black mustard seeds
8–10 curry leaves
3 cloves of garlic, cut into large slivers
2 large ripe tomatoes, roughly chopped
¾ tsp red chilli powder
1 tsp ground cumin
1 tsp dried fenugreek leaves (methi)
¾ tsp salt
200g cooked basmati rice

Put a large pan on medium-high heat and add the coconut or vegetable oil. When it is hot, add the mustard seeds, curry leaves and garlic and fry, stirring well, for 1–2 minutes. Add the tomatoes, all the other spices and salt then stir well. Cook for 5–10 minutes, or until the tomatoes are soft and disintegrating. Turn the heat down and tip in the cooked rice. Mix well to amalgamate all the flavours and ensure the rice is really heated through. Serve piping hot.

Variation:

Sumati makes yoghurt rice in the summer, when she likes something cooling. She fries ½ teaspoon of mustard seeds with ½ teaspoon ground cumin, 2 teaspoons each of urad dal and chana dal, 4–5 peppercorns, a handful of curry leaves and 1 or 2 split whole green chillies. When fragrant, she turns off the gas and stirs in 100g plain yoghurt and 200g freshly cooked rice.

Lemon rice

MUTHULAXMI, MEMBER OF WOMEN'S GROUP AT KANAK DURGA SLUM

Muthulaxmi makes this southern Indian rice dish for breakfast-on-the-go when she takes the long train ride back to her village. She eats it with coconut chutney or spicy tomato pickle. My maternal grandparents (one of whom was born in Calcutta) sometimes served kedgeree for breakfast, which was a favourite during childhood visits. This lovely, pale yellow, fragrant dish also works beautifully alongside curry dishes for lunch or supper.

SERVES 3–4

200g basmati rice
1 tbsp vegetable oil
½ tsp black mustard seeds
1 tsp chana dal
6–8 dried or fresh curry leaves
2–4 dried red chillies (optional)
Juice of 1 large lemon
½ tsp ground turmeric
Salt to taste
Fresh coriander leaves to
    garnish

Measure the dry rice in a jug and note the volume. Wash the rice in a sieve under cold water, until the water runs clear. Put the rice in a large pan (one that has a well-fitting lid) with double the volume of water and bring to the boil. Cover, lower the heat to minimum and cook for 8–10 minutes until the water has been absorbed. Set aside.

Heat the oil in a karhai or large saute pan; when it is hot, add the mustard seeds, chana dal, curry leaves and red chillies (if using) and stir around in the hot oil until aromatic and sizzling (1–2 minutes). Take off the heat for a minute, then add in the lemon juice, ground turmeric and salt and stir well (being careful as it can spit). Put it back on the heat, mix in 2 tablespoons of boiling water, then fold in the cooked hot rice. Serve garnished with coriander leaves.

Variation:

Alternatively, cook the rice in the same pan as the spices: fry the seeds, dal and spices as above, and once sizzling add the drained, uncooked rice with the turmeric. Add the measured amount of boiling water to the pan (double the rice by volume) then cover and cook on low for 10 minutes. Stir in the lemon juice, add garnish and fluff up the rice to serve.

breads

Hina, Seelampur

Hina is a gracious woman in her early twenties with long, slender hands and a gentle demeanour. She has a way of making friends despite our language barrier. We take ourselves off to a quiet corner, away from the sound of the centre's generator and the women discussing the making of bread. I hear her story in exactly her own words: she is one of the few to talk to us without an interpreter. I discover she is determined to impact the world for good.

She began attending Asha's children's groups at the age of five. Now an undergraduate, she visits Seelampur's Asha centre several times a week to help younger students with their homework and career planning. A year ago she interned with the Australian High Commission in New Delhi through Asha's internship programme. I joked that she sounds too busy to sleep: she replied that she manages five hours a night!

Hina volunteers with Asha as a teacher in the settlement at 'New Seelampur', where resourceful and resilient refugees from Bihar are living in makeshift shelters on a floodplain under a motorway flyover. When we visited, we found her teaching a class sitting on the wiry grass. She was handing out exercise books to a group of children who seemed to us about four-to-eight years old, but were actually older. She teaches them English and history, watched as well by the community's goats. Despite the limited teaching materials, she held the children's attention brilliantly.

She told me that her father is a rickshaw puller and she has seven siblings. Her mother started teaching her to cook when she was 12 years old, and because she loves doing it, Hina cooks for her family every day after college. All this, while studying in a highly competitive environment, reading Urdu at Delhi University. Within Asha, she is a Student Ambassador, which means she is responsible for mentoring younger students. Sometimes, Hina is also called upon to share with wider audiences the message of what Asha can achieve if others will support them.

She is keen to give credit to Asha: her written tribute is displayed on the noticeboard at Seelampur and bubbles up in our conversation too. 'Whatever I am, it is because of Asha. Because of Asha I have confidence. If I'm speaking to you, it's because of Asha. My studies are because of Asha. I had a fear of speaking in public. I was not expected to have a voice outside the family, but here I learnt to speak in public.' I ask her what she wants to do in the future. 'I want to be an Urdu language professor. I hope to give back double what I've been given.'

Layered paratha

HINA, STUDENT AMBASSADOR AT SEELAMPUR SLUM

Hina deftly demonstrated this stunning bread for us, her slender fingers working the dough with gentle authority. Bread-making is something she does every day, like many Indian women, and you could tell that as she worked: chatting happily to us, she barely looked at what she was doing as she divided and shaped the dough into balls. The secret to the layered, flaky texture of these gorgeous parathas is the clever rolling and coiling of the dough. It's not something most of us will be used to doing, but it's not intrinsically complicated either. I have really enjoyed learning to make these and I do recommend you give it a go. Hina says the addition of semolina accentuates the pinwheel pattern of these layers, but these will still work brilliantly without it.

MAKES 8–10

400g chapatti flour (*atta*) or stoneground wholewheat flour
2 tbsp vegetable oil
1 tsp semolina (optional)
Salt to taste
Vegetable oil or ghee for frying

Make the paratha dough: put the flour and semolina into a large bowl with a pinch of salt. Drizzle over the vegetable oil and rub it in with your fingers. Put 220–300ml tepid water in a jug, then add it 2–3 tablespoons at a time until you have a soft, slightly sticky dough that forms a ball. You may not need all the water. Knead the dough on a lightly floured surface for 8–10 minutes until it is no longer sticky, but smooth and elastic. Put it back in the bowl, cover with cling film or a tea towel and leave to rest for 15 minutes.

Divide the dough into 8–10 small balls. Take one ball and roll it out on a lightly floured surface into a thin disc about 20cm across. Brush the paratha with a very thin layer of vegetable oil, then starting at one side of the disc, roll it up tightly into a thin sausage. Coil this up into a spiral (like a snail shell), lay it down then flatten gently with your fingers before rolling it out again to a disc 2–3mm thick. Repeat with the other balls of dough.

Heat a tawa or small frying pan over a high heat until it is really hot. Put a paratha in the pan and cook for a couple of minutes until the surface starts to bubble. Flip it over, then coat the top with oil or melted ghee with the back of a teaspoon. Flip it again and coat the second side, then continue turning it for another minute on each side until it is golden with brown patches. Keep it warm or wrap with foil whilst you make the rest of the parathas.

Serve hot with chutneys, pickles or raita, or as part of a main meal.

Bajra ki roti

SANTOSH, COOK FOR DR KIRAN AND FREDDY MARTIN

As Victoria eats gluten free, Santosh made these delicious, nutty wheat-free breads for us for breakfast everyday. Delicious with eggs, simply with butter or as an accompaniment to a main meal, they are tasty and versatile. Santosh is a fabulous cook and she showed us that this rougher millet dough needs careful handling to prevent it from cracking as it is shaped. Don't let that put you off though. They taste wholesome and nutty with little bursts of chilli and coriander, and no-one will mind if they are not formed into perfect circles.

MAKES 4–5

6 heaped tbsp millet flour, with extra for rolling out (bajri flour)

Salt to taste

1 tbsp vegetable oil plus more for frying

Milk (ideally at room temperature)

3 heaped tbsp red onion, very finely chopped

½ tsp very finely chopped thin green chilli

1–2 tbsp fresh coriander, finely chopped

Make the dough: put the flour into a large bowl with a pinch of salt and make a well in the middle. Put 1 tablespoon of oil in the well, then slowly add milk, 1–2 tablespoons at a time, until you have a soft, slightly sticky dough that forms a ball. Add the onion, chilli and fresh coriander and knead the dough on a lightly floured surface for a minute until it is no longer sticky, but is firm and smooth. Cover the bowl with cling film or a damp tea towel whilst you make the roti.

Divide the dough into 4–5 golf-ball sized balls. Take a ball and dip it into millet flour so it is lightly coated. With your fingers, pat it into a thin disc about 2–3mm thick, on a lightly floured surface. Every so often, cup your hands around the sides of the disc and turn the dough to encourage it back into a smooth circle. Alternatively, roll it very lightly, possibly between sheets of greaseproof paper, into a rough circle. Be careful not to be too firm or it may well crack. Repeat with the other balls of dough.

Heat a tawa or small frying pan over a high heat until it is really hot. Put a roti in the pan and cook for a 30 seconds. Flip it over, then lightly coat the cooked side with oil or melted ghee with the back of a teaspoon. Flip it over and coat the second side, then continue flipping for another minute on each side until it is golden with brown patches. Keep it warm or wrap with foil whilst you make the rest of the rotis. Serve hot.

Variation:

Omit the onion, chilli and coriander for a plain version you can eat with sweet toppings. I have it on good authority they are delicious spread with Nutella.

Makki ki roti

Another gluten-free alternative uses cornmeal instead of millet flour. Use the same quantity of fine cornmeal, salt, onion and optional chilli, then make into a soft dough adding water until it forms a firm, non-sticky dough. Knead for a minute then form into balls and proceed as above.

Spinach paratha

MAMTA, MEMBER OF WOMEN'S GROUP AT KALKAJI SLUM

Mamta's parathas looked tasty and wholesome: golden flatbreads generously flecked with vivid green, as if they would do you good whilst tasting delicious at the same time. Mamta made them with fenugreek leaves (methi), but we have used baby spinach instead which gives a similar appearance. Dressed in a beautiful green embroidered salwar kameez, Mamta could not have picked a better backdrop for her lovely plate of parathas.

MAKES 10–12

250g stoneground wholewheat flour (chapatti flour or atta)

100g baby spinach, washed and dried

1 medium red onion, very finely chopped

2–3 thin green chillies, very finely chopped

2 sprigs fresh coriander, finely chopped

¼ tsp carom seeds

¼ tsp grated root ginger

Salt to taste

Vegetable oil or ghee for frying

Make the paratha dough: put the flour into a large bowl with a pinch of salt. Put 150–170ml of tepid water in a jug, then add it 2–3 tablespoonfuls at a time until you have a soft, slightly sticky dough that forms a ball. You may not need all the water. Knead the dough on a lightly floured surface for 5–8 minutes until it is no longer sticky, but is smooth and pliable. Put it back in the bowl, cover with cling film or a tea towel and leave to rest for 15 minutes.

Ensure the spinach is dry, then chop very finely and mix with all the other ingredients in a small bowl. Once the dough has finished resting, add the vegetable-spice mix into it and knead again until it is evenly incorporated. Divide the dough into 10–12 small balls.

Heat a tawa or small frying pan over a high heat until it is really hot. Roll out a ball of dough to a small disc about 3–4 mm thick. Put it in the pan and cook for 2 minutes on each side, coating each side once with oil or melted ghee with the back of a teaspoon when you flip it over. Repeat for another minute on each side until golden with brown patches. Keep it warm or wrap with foil whilst you make the rest of the parathas.

Serve hot with chutneys, pickles or raita, or as part of a main meal.

Radha, Trilokpuri

Radha's red bangles pick up the colours of her sari. She is rolling out wheat dough for her parathas. Colleagues are asking her questions about her recipe and she answers in a soft, warm voice.

One of the joys of this trip has been watching women's hands form all manner of breads with great precision. They produce everything from plain flatbreads to complicated stuffed parathas, at a speed that makes the process look more like a party trick than a chore. They have honed their skills with years of hard work. Radha gained her expertise feeding her family of seven.

She presses, knuckles and regathers her mixture with one hand as the other steadies the shallow metal dish. She pulls off a lump of dough and forms it into a little bowl in the cupped palm of her hand. She fills it with spicy onions, pinches it closed and squashes her artwork down on the board. She

rolls it out again, this time it is studded with the colourful ingredients and ready for the hot oil. Her bangles are clinking as she works, punctuating the chatter of the women around us.

We ask Radha what difference Asha has made to her life. Her voice quietens and she stares into the middle distance: 'Before, I didn't go out,' she said, 'I was under the veil; I didn't speak to people. Now I am open to any conversation. It would take me three days to tell you all of the changes that have happened to me!'

'For one thing,' she smiles, 'I didn't know about family planning when we had kids. I would not have had so many children but I was told to have more by my mother-in-law. As a daughter-in-law I didn't have any say in the matter.' Since then things have changed for Radha. She trained as an Asha Community Health Volunteer and has served as such for 12 years. One of her tasks is to help families navigate the complexities of family planning.

Radha's husband has seen the benefit of Asha's support for his family. When his employer owed him money for three months' work, Radha and other women from Asha's women's group went to her husband's workplace and convinced the boss to pay the wages owed. Now if her husband has a problem with something, he comes to her. He's very proud of her.

We express our admiration at Radha's courage. She credits Sweeta, her inspirational Asha team leader. 'Sweeta has been there all this time, like a mother guiding us,' she smiles. 'I feel sad if I don't see her for long so I call her up!' Our conversation turns to the future. Radha tells us, 'Asha has taught me about saving money. I arranged a loan from Asha's Financial Inclusion Programme and bought two plots of land for my family. I've repaid the loan too.' With support, Radha has been able to give her family greater resilience to whatever life throws at them.

Onion paratha

RADHA, COMMUNITY HEALTH VOLUNTEER AT TRILOKPURI SLUM

Quietly confident with a steady gaze, Radha was delighted to show us how to make her onion flatbreads. We watched, enchanted, as she made each ball of dough into the cutest little cup, ready to receive its pretty pink onion filling. The end result was super tasty: golden, buttery onion bread with a noticeable hint of chilli. I wish we could have had longer to sample her full range of stuffed parathas. She said she makes variations with cauliflower, spiced mashed potato, grated radish, fenugreek leaves and grated paneer. They are popular for breakfast or with main meals to mop up sauces or scoop up mouthfuls.

MAKES 6

250g chapatti flour (*atta*) or stoneground wholewheat flour

Salt to taste

1 tbsp vegetable oil

1 medium red onion, very finely chopped

1–4 thin green chillies, very finely chopped

¼ tsp nigella seeds

Vegetable oil or ghee for frying

Make the paratha dough: put the flour into a large bowl with a pinch of salt. Drizzle in the vegetable oil and rub it in with your fingers. Put 150–170ml of tepid water in a jug then add it 2–3 tablespoons at a time until you have a soft, slightly sticky dough that forms a ball. You may not need all the water. Knead the dough on a lightly floured surface for 8–10 minutes until it is no longer sticky, but smooth and elastic. Put it back in the bowl, cover with cling film or a tea towel and leave to rest for 15 minutes.

Mix the onion, chillies and nigella seeds together in a bowl or on a plate. Divide the dough into 6 small balls. Take one ball and form it into a little cup in the palm of your hand. Fill it with a sixth of the onion-chilli mix and encase the dough around it again, to form a ball. On a lightly floured surface, roll out the ball to form a disc about 3mm thick. Repeat with the other balls of dough. Lay the rolled-out parathas on greaseproof paper to prevent them sticking to each other.

Heat a tawa or small frying pan over a high heat until it is really hot. Put a paratha in the pan and cook for a couple of minutes until the surface starts to bubble. Flip it over then coat the top with oil or melted ghee with the back of a teaspoon. Repeat and coat the second side, then keep flipping the bread for another minute on each side until it is golden with brown patches. Keep it warm or wrap with foil whilst you make the rest of the parathas.

Serve hot with chutneys, pickles or raita, or as part of a main meal.

Variation:

Beena (a staff member at Zakhira slum) also cooked these for us. Her recipe included ¼ tsp *amchoor* (dried mango powder), ½ tsp red chilli powder, 1 tsp ground coriander and some fresh coriander in the filling with the onions and chilli. Both are equally delicious, just different.

Pea poori

MANU, ASHA STAFF AT KALKAJI SLUM

I had never eaten freshly-made pooris before Manu made them for us and they were memorable. She created these light, puffy, golden breads with their hidden green middles with such ease. Hot from the karhai, these soft pillows of deliciousness are rather addictive; at least they are small enough that you can have two or three without feeling too guilty! Manu's gold earrings danced as her hands expertly kneaded, rolled, cupped, filled and flipped the pale glossy dough. We were clearly watching an expert at work. Don't be put off if it sounds complicated – it is well worth the effort and the hot oil does the magical bit at the end anyway. These are delicious served with chutneys as a snack, or as part of any Indian meal.

MAKES 20+

350g plain flour or chapatti flour (atta)
2 tbsp vegetable oil
½ tsp salt
300g frozen peas
35g root ginger, peeled and roughly chopped
3 thin green chillies, roughly chopped
¼ tsp carom seeds (if you have them)
4–5 stems fresh coriander
500ml vegetable oil for deep frying

Make the poori dough: put the flour into a large bowl with the salt. Add one tablespoon of vegetable oil and mix it into the dough to form crumbs. Add tepid water bit by bit until you have a soft dough that forms a ball and does not stick to your fingers. Knead the dough on a lightly floured surface for 5–10 minutes until it is smooth, springy and pliable.

Cook the peas with the ginger and chillies in boiling water until tender. Drain and tip into a blender with one tablespoon of oil, the carom seeds and fresh coriander. Pulse until you have a coarse paste, then season. Don't be tempted to add water, you need a dryish mixture.

Tear off small sections of dough the size of a large cherry tomato and with oiled hands shape into small balls. Take one ball and shape it into a small cup in the palm of your hand. Put a teaspoonful of the pea filling in the middle, then crimp the edges back together to form a sealed parcel. Roll this out very gently on a lightly floured surface into a disc about 8–9 cm across. Repeat with the other balls of dough.

Pour vegetable oil into a karhai or medium-sized pan to a depth of about 6cm (making sure it is not more than a third full for safety). Place it over a high heat until it is really hot. Drop in a flat poori disc, gently holding it down in the oil with a slotted spoon as it puffs up. Once golden, flip it over and cook the other side until that too is puffy with small bubbles on the surface. Drain on kitchen paper, then keep warm wrapped in foil whilst you make the rest of the pooris, or serve them as they are ready. (Note that the pooris will only puff up if they are submerged and the oil is hot enough.)

accompaniments

Madhuri, Kanak Durga

Madhuri is a quiet, friendly young student who comes across as a very practical person. We're meeting her at the Asha centre that serves the slum of Kanak Durga, where she lives with her family among about 3,000 other residents. She is showing us how to make one of the key additions to an Indian meal, a yoghurt side dish called a raita, which is particularly useful for its ability to cool the effects of chilli. She's generous with her information, telling us how the recipe can be altered to suit different members of her family.

Madhuri likes cooking so she and her mother share the food preparation at home. Handling this alongside her studies, she says, is all about time management. She offers us a taste of the raita and tells us how she loves a little bowl of it at the end of a meal, whereas her sister and her mother prefer it served with the rest of the food. Indians use a raita as a palate-cleanser. She gives us a little insight into the importance of a raita in an Indian meal. 'People like to have this with dal and chapatti,' she explains, 'but it doesn't go with okra: it would ruin its taste.'

Her ease with sharing information is a natural gift that she is hoping to turn into a career. Madhuri is in her final year at university on a combined bachelor of arts degree (the BA Programme) and hopes to pursue a masters' degree in Mass Communication. This would involve learning about editing and journalism together with skills for TV, such as anchoring and hosting. Mass media is accessible to people in slums more than ever before. One of Madhuri's favourite family meals now is an Italian recipe she came across because of access to the internet.

Many homes have televisions, if few other luxuries. Some residents now have mobile phones, including smartphones, but computers have always been unaffordable for them. Several of the young people we met mentioned that they had never seen a computer before they came into the Asha centre. Asha has recently invited donations of used laptops for the use of its students in higher education. These days, computers are an essential tool for undertaking university coursework.

Madhuri's parents fully support her continuing in education. She explains, 'My mother only got to Fifth Class at school so she has wanted me to continue my studies.' This means her mother finished her education around the age of 10. Her father is an electrician. Madhuri is the eldest of five children and as a first-generation college student has benefitted from Asha's resourceful support for students. Madhuri is broadening her horizons already and hopes to enter an industry that enables individuals to impact the world.

Cucumber raita

MADHURI, STUDENT AT KANAK DURGA SLUM

Although this is a simple dish, Madhuri prepared it for us with such enthusiasm. With bright eyes and a big smile, she explained that she likes to eat this on its own at the end of a meal, especially in the heat of summer when it is deliciously cooling and refreshing. Her mother and sister prefer to have it as an accompaniment to dry vegetable dishes, rice and dal. Either way, it is a classic component of an Indian meal that is a great foil to the other complex spices and flavours.

SERVES 4–5

400g plain yoghurt
½ cucumber, peeled and grated
¾ tsp salt
Ground black pepper
½ tsp ground cumin
2 pinches red chilli powder

Put the yoghurt into a mixing bowl and add the grated cucumber. (I like to leave the peel on for extra colour, and prefer to squeeze the excess water from the cucumber first. To do this, lay a double thickness of kitchen roll in a sieve and add the grated cucumber. Leave for 10 minutes, then gather up the corners of the kitchen roll and squeeze out as much of the liquid as you can. This is optional: I know Madhuri prefers a runnier raita!) Mix well.

Add the salt, black pepper and ground cumin and stir well. Sprinkle the chilli powder on top as a garnish. Cover and chill in the fridge until ready to serve.

Variation: Mixed raita

Follow the recipe above, replacing the grated cucumber with an equal mix of finely diced red onion, tomato and cucumber.

Mint raita

SWEETA, SUPERVISOR OF ASHA'S WORK IN MULTIPLE SLUMS

Sweeta explained that this raita is a family favourite that she learnt from her daughter, who in turn learnt it from her aunt. I love the way women pass on recipes to each other and I do the same in my family. Some are simply emailed these days, but the best ones we learn watching over the shoulder of a cook we admire. This raita is creamy, refreshing with the mint, and has a lovely garlicky flavour that goes brilliantly with lamb dishes. Sweeta says she also eats it with pakoras, fried fish or fried chicken dishes, and that it's good for the digestion.

SERVES 4–5

400g plain yoghurt
Small bunch of fresh mint,
    leaves only
4–5 sprigs of fresh coriander
5 cloves garlic, peeled and
    roughly chopped
2 thin green chillies (optional)
¾ tsp salt

Put the yoghurt into a bowl. Put all the other ingredients into a blender and whizz together with half a small glass of water. (Don't be tempted to add the yoghurt as well, it will make it too runny.) Add this puree to the yoghurt and mix well. Cover and chill in the fridge until ready to serve.

Boondi raita

UJALA, HOUSEKEEPER FOR DR KIRAN & FREDDY MARTIN

Ujala looked after us beautifully when we stayed with Dr Kiran and Freddy whilst researching this book. She packed us goodie bags of fruit to take with us each day and always gave us such a welcome when we returned home tired, our heads full of stories and with notebooks bursting with new dishes. We had fun exchanging recipes too: we cooked shepherd's pie and apple crumble and she cooked a myriad of delicious things. This raita made with *boondi* (little balls of deep-fried gram flour) is a house speciality and well worth making if you can track down the *boondi*.

SERVES 4–5

400g plain yoghurt
2–3 tbsp icing sugar
4–5 pinches salt
5 heaped tbsp *boondi*
Fresh coriander to garnish

Put the yoghurt into a bowl. Whisk in the sugar and salt; taste, to check it seems balanced. Whisk in water until you have the consistency of single cream. Cover and chill in the fridge until ready to serve.

Just before serving, stir in the *boondi* and the fresh coriander. Doing this at the last minute keeps the texture of the boondi quite crunchy. If you prefer a softer texture, add the *boondi* 15–30 minutes before eating, during which time they will absorb some of the liquid and become much softer.

Variation:

Add 1 teaspoon of toasted ground cumin, ½ tsp red chilli powder and a grind of black pepper, if you want to up the spice level of this gentle, soothing raita.

Walnut chutney

SHABNAM, ASHA COMMUNICATIONS TEAM MEMBER

Shabnam explained that this chutney is a Kashmiri speciality made with local walnuts, which grow in abundance in the region. Traditionally it would have been ground by hand – without yoghurt – in a pestle and mortar, giving a pesto-like texture. Her version was thin, smooth and creamy; blend it for as long or as little as you want to achieve the texture you like. It is always served at weddings in Kashmir and is definitely worth trying for its spicy, nutty, minty taste. Shabnam recommends using it instead of mayo in sandwiches, as well as to accompany Indian dishes.

SERVES 6

1 cup plain yoghurt
1 cup walnut halves
1–3 thin green chillies, finely
  chopped
2–3 stems fresh mint, leaves
  picked and chopped, plus
  more for garnishing
Salt

Put the yoghurt into a blender with all the other ingredients. Whizz until the walnuts are very finely chopped and the mixture is almost smooth. Serve immediately or cover and chill until needed. It will keep for 3–4 days in the fridge. Garnish with fresh mint before serving.

Variation:

There are many versions of this chutney: some add 1–2 cloves of garlic and toasted cumin seeds, if you want to ring the changes.

Coriander chutney

ANITA, TEAM LEADER AT CHANDERPURI SLUM

The Asha centre in Chanderpuri slum is just beyond a very big rubbish dump. Not the nicest of locations, yet once we crossed the concrete yard and went through the entrance, all of that was forgotten as we met Anita and her team. Anita made this as an accompaniment to some chickpea kebabs she cooked and served for us; yet it was the vibrant green colour and zingy taste of this chutney that stole the show. Versions of this recipe duly appeared very regularly throughout our trip, as fresh chutneys such as this are a common feature of everyday Indian meals.

SERVES 4–5

1 small bunch fresh coriander, roughly chopped

2 cloves garlic, peeled and roughly chopped

2 thin green chillies, roughly chopped

1 tomato, roughly chopped

Salt to taste

Put all the ingredients into a food processor or blender with 3–4 tablespoons water and whizz until smooth. Adjust seasoning to taste, cover and chill in the fridge until ready to serve. Use within 2–3 days.

Variation: Coriander and mint chutney

Follow the recipe above, adding the leaves from 4–5 stems of fresh mint. Some people like to add 2–3 teaspoons fresh lime juice instead of some of the water. Another cook used a little water to create a coarse paste, and then the chutney was thinned to a runny, dip-like consistency with natural yoghurt. Ring the changes as you want, depending on your mood or what you are pairing it with. It's a bit like gravy for us…the possibilities and subtleties are endless!

Tomato chutney

SAROJ, TEAM LEADER AT TRILOKPURI SLUM

Saroj makes this tomato chutney often because she says it tastes so good. She is animated as she tells us it gives *chatkara* (a smack) in her mouth. In other words this vibrant, fresh chutney adds a burst of flavour to whatever it accompanies. Although it is called tomato chutney, it may appear green when made due to the abundance of coriander. If you want a more obviously tomatoey version, feel free to reduce the coriander.

SERVES 4–5

½–¾ small bunch fresh coriander, roughly chopped

4 cloves garlic, peeled and roughly chopped

2–4 thin green chillies, roughly chopped

4 large ripe tomatoes, roughly chopped

2 pinches asafoetida (if you have it)

Salt to taste

Put all the ingredients into a food processor or blender with 1–2 tablespoons water and whizz until you have a grainy, pesto-style texture. Adjust seasoning to taste, cover and chill in the fridge until ready to serve. Use within 2–3 days.

Variation:

If your tomatoes are not super ripe, add a teaspoon of soft brown sugar. Experiment with substituting lime juice as all or part of the liquid. Add more or less chilli to suit your taste.

drinks & desserts

Gulab jamun

SAMINA, MIDWIFE AT SEELAMPUR SLUM

Whenever I see Samina, I am guaranteed one of her twinkly-eyed smiles and utterly embracing hugs. Visiting her home for the first time was a really moving experience. The team and I climbed up the steep, narrow stairs to her room, where we were welcomed by Samina and her ten children. She motioned to her eldest son to turn on the rusted ceiling fan. The electrics looked dangerous and I tried to communicate that we were fine without it. Samina insisted, so he gave it a sharp prod to get it turning…at which point, to our astonishment, the most beautiful cascade of deep-pink rose petals showered our heads! Samina had painstakingly lined each blade with them to create the most special welcome I have ever received. Six years later, I cradled her baby grandchild in my arms and ate these incredible gulab jamun. Appropriately, *gulab* means 'rose' in Hindi, and with these soft, light, syrupy spheres, Samina had served up another memorable experience!

SERVES 4–5

2 litres full-fat milk
250g caster sugar
250ml water
100g plain flour
½ tsp bicarbonate of soda
1 litre vegetable oil for deep
    frying

Start by making the reduced milk paste, or *khoya*, that gives these balls such a great taste. Put the milk in a large non-stick saucepan or high-sided frying pan. Bring it to the boil, turn the heat down and simmer gently, stirring regularly until the milk begins to thicken and turn golden and creamy. After about 40 minutes, the milk will have evaporated and reduced and will be starting to solidify. With a spatula, scrape back into the mixture the solids that are exposed around the edge. Continue stirring until the milk has formed a grainy, cottage-cheese-like paste and no further bubbles are visible on the surface. This could take another 20–30 minutes, or more depending on the level of heat and width of the pan. Transfer to a bowl and leave to cool. (You can prepare this in advance and leave it covered in the fridge for up to 2 days. However, it may solidify on overnight chilling, in which case stir it well or grate it and add a splash of milk to soften it and re-create the paste-like texture before using it.)

Make the sugar syrup. Put the sugar and the water in a saucepan and bring to the boil over a high heat, stirring until all the sugar crystals dissolve. Turn the heat down and simmer for about 10 minutes until you have a clear, syrupy texture. Take it off the heat and leave to one side.

Next make the gulab jamun dough. Once the milk paste has cooled, knead it gently in a large mixing bowl until smooth. Add the flour and bicarbonate

of soda and knead just until it has combined to form a soft dough. Roll into equally sized balls no bigger than a cherry tomato, as they will expand when fried. Make them as smooth and crack-free as you can. (Add a dab of oil to your hands to help with this if needed.) Leave to one side.

Put the oil in a deep-sided saucepan (no more than a third full) over a high heat until very hot. Test it with a ball or bit of the dough; it should rise bubbling to the surface in a few seconds. Fry the balls in batches of about six, for 4–6 minutes, turning half way though, until golden brown and cooked through. Lift out with a slotted spoon and place into the warm sugar syrup. Leave them to soak up some of the syrup for 10–15 minutes. Serve each person a ball or two, warm, in a few spoonfuls of the syrup.

Variation:

In India the sugar syrup is often flavoured with rosewater: add 1–2 tsp rosewater to the syrup once it is made and serve the soaked balls lightly sprinkled with finely crushed pistachios. Alternatively, serve with vanilla ice-cream.

Shortcuts:

You can make them in advance, refrigerating them until needed, in which case reheat gently before serving. Instead of making the milk paste (*khoya*), you can use 250g milk powder mixed with 6–7 tbsp condensed milk to form a thick paste.

Snehlata, Mayapuri

of colours', when strangers in the street celebrate by throwing powder paint at one another.

Snehlata and her painter husband come from Bihar province. I ask her how she finds life in Delhi compared to home. 'Most women wear the veil in Bihar,' she says, and explains that she has more freedom here in Delhi. 'We are of a high caste, so my husband's work would be considered shameful; we would be outcasts if this were known back home.' Our interpreter explains that they are of the pandit caste: the men are traditionally expected to serve as priests in the temples. However, Snehlata sees society changing. 'The older generation live by the caste system,' she says, 'my generation have dispensed with that.' We still see evidence of it during our trip, but we also hear of Asha encouraging the women to see beyond caste. Asha encourages everyone in the community centres to eat their meals together, something they would never have done otherwise as it means sharing food with people of a different caste. One team leader remembers the day she mixed up all the chapattis so no-one could tell whose was whose, and they saw that bread was bread, whoever had cooked it.

In her high, clear voice Snehlata explains that she loves to serve people now as a Community Health Volunteer. She originally came to Asha because the charity provided a dispensary service and she needed to arrange immunisation for her children. That was 12 years ago and the family has since participated in the children's and women's groups that Asha run. Coming to live in Mayapuri meant mixing with people from all kinds of backgrounds and Snehlata explains that working with Asha has taught her something that means a lot to her. 'As pandits, my family would not mix with people of lower castes, but here I've discovered that we are all the same.' Snehlata makes her way around the room offering sweet aromatic fritters to the rest of the group. One of her friends whispers to us a little Hindi lesson: '*sneh* is the word for love.'

Snehlata is a wife and mother in Mayapuri slum. She has been a longstanding member of the women's group and is now an Asha Community Health Volunteer. She has an open, peaceful face as she shares with us her own experience of one of India's big social issues.

She moved to Delhi with her husband 12 years ago and he found work with a small outfit of painters and polishers. When it became clear they were not giving him a fair wage, he struck out on his own as a house painter. House walls in every slum are painted in a variety of attractive colours, giving them a beauty that contrasts with the widespread hardships of life within. I imagine his work clothes display a delightful range of colourful paint-drips. Snehlata serves us a tray of the most delicious banana fritters. She explains that she makes them for Holi, the 'feast

Banana fritters

SNEHLATA, COMMUNITY HEALTH VOLUNTEER AT MAYAPURI SLUM

This dessert has been passed down the generations in Snehlata's family. It is always served at festivals, but also when they just want something sweet with a cup of chai. These light, golden, crispy-on-the-outside-soft-in-the-middle fritters are totally delicious and incredibly moreish. Made with ripe bananas, coconut and subtly spiced with cardamom and fennel, they taste both exotic and very comforting at the same time. Serve as a pudding with vanilla or salted caramel ice-cream; or sprinkle with caster sugar and serve with tea. Do consider halving the recipe for fewer people, as this quantity does make a lot of batter.

SERVES 8–10

500ml full-fat milk

2 very ripe bananas

50g freshly grated coconut or desiccated coconut (soaked in water for 15 mins then drained)

250g semolina

250g plain flour (or rice flour)

400g caster sugar

25g dates, very finely chopped (optional)

Seeds of 5 green cardamom pods, finely crushed

1 tbsp fennel seeds, finely ground

500ml vegetable oil for deep frying

Put the milk in a large bowl, add a small cup of water. Mash the bananas in another bowl with the coconut and stir the mixture gradually into the milk. Add all the other dry ingredients, fruit and spices and stir gently until you have a smooth batter. Cover and leave to rest for 2 hours, so the flavours develop and the batter thickens slightly.

Put the oil in a deep-sided saucepan (no more than a third full) over a high heat until very hot. Using a small ladle or serving spoon, pour spoonfuls of the batter into the hot oil. Cook in batches of 4 or 5 at a time, until each fritter is golden brown (about 2 minutes on each side). Remove with a slotted spoon and drain on a plate covered with kitchen roll.

Serve warm, sprinkled with more caster sugar if desired.

Carrot halwa

ZAINAB, COLLEGE STUDENT FROM SEELAMPUR SLUM

Zainab is a proud 2nd-year BA Programme student who hopes to become a social worker. In her community, girls are usually married by the age of 20 with only a basic education behind them and no career prospects ahead of them, so she is acutely aware of the opportunity Asha has given her. She explained that she loves to cook, but has little time. Her father has a vegetable cart, so she made this dish for us with fresh bottle gourd (*lauki*). When we looked blank, she laughed and said it was just as delicious made with carrots! Unsure of carrots as a dessert? Think carrot cake but more exotic: this is a meltingly soft, sticky pudding with a golden orange glow and a subtle hint of cardamom.

SERVES 6

2 tbsp ghee or butter
500g carrots, peeled and finely grated
200g caster sugar
200ml full-fat milk
¼ tsp ground cardamom (or ground seeds from 5–8 cardamom pods)
1 tbsp chopped or grated fresh coconut (optional)

Garnish:

Any or all of the following:
1 tbsp desiccated coconut
1 tbsp chopped whole almonds
1 tbsp chopped raw cashew nuts
1 tbsp unsalted peanuts
1 tbsp sultanas

Melt the butter or ghee in a large pan over a highish heat, then add the grated carrots and stir well for 5 minutes.

Add the sugar, milk and ground cardamom, reduce the heat to low and cook until the carrots are meltingly soft, the liquid has evaporated and it smells sweet and caramelised. (If using the chopped fresh coconut, add it once the liquid is reduced by half.) Keep an eye on it and stir as needed to stop the mixture catching on the bottom of the pan. This could take up to an hour, depending on the size of your pan and how finely the carrots are grated.

Enjoy warm in small bowls, garnished with as many of the toppings as you want.

Variation:

For a richer, more indulgent treat, replace all of the milk with condensed milk (and reduce the sugar by up to half), or simply stir 1–2 tbsp condensed milk in with the sugar.

If you do use grated bottle gourd, put it in a wide, shallow pan by itself over a lowish heat and evaporate the water for 10 minutes before following the recipe above.

Great with:

Vanilla ice cream

Gujiya

RAMKALI, COMMUNITY HEALTH VOLUNTEER AT JEEWAN NAGAR SLUM

I was absolutely enchanted by gujiya, both eating them and watching Ramkali expertly make them. They are small, crisp, half-moon shaped pastries, filled with a sweet mixture of nuts and coconut. Freshly cooked, they melt in the mouth, taste exotic and are extremely moreish. Ramkali explained that they are made throughout India for festivals, especially Holi, Diwali and Christmas. In usage and format, they remind me of mince pies, but have a more delicate flavour. Regional variations exist: sometimes cinnamon, poppy seeds, raisins or crushed green cardamom seeds are added to the filling. If you like pastry, these are fun to make. Ramkali used a special mould (like an empañada mould) to shape and fill them, but they work just as well made free-form with a crimped edge. It may be gilding the lily, but I would be tempted to dust these with caster sugar once fried, both for sparkle and crunch.

SERVES 12

200g plain flour, plus extra for dusting
1 tbsp oil or melted butter
1–2 tbsp desiccated coconut
5–7 tbsp chopped mixed nuts (e.g. almonds, cashews and pistachios)
6 tbsp caster sugar, with more for sprinkling
100g khoya (grated or crumbled) (see gulab jamun recipe, page 164)
Vegetable oil for deep frying

Put the flour into a bowl and add the melted butter or oil. Add 100–125ml cold water, a little at a time, to make a firm dough. Tip it onto a floured work surface and knead for 5 minutes or so until it is soft, pliable but not sticky. Set aside, back in the bowl, covered with a tea towel.

Make the filling by mixing the coconut, chopped nuts, sugar and khoya in a bowl. If you are using condensed milk, use the greater amount of coconut and nuts to absorb some of the moisture. You are aiming for a firm paste-like texture. Set aside.

Divide the dough into 12 and roll into balls. With a rolling pin, roll each ball into a small disc about 1mm thick. Place a twelfth of the filling on one half of the disc, leaving the edges bare. Wet the edges of the pastry with your finger dipped into cold water, then fold over the circle to form a Cornish pasty shape. Press the edges tightly together, then crimp with a fork or fold over repeatedly into a pretty scalloped edge. Repeat with the remaining pastry balls and filling, placing the formed pastries on a lightly floured surface.

Heat enough oil to fill a pan no more than one third full. When really hot, deep fry the pastries for 1–2 minutes on each side until crisp and golden brown. Drain on kitchen paper, sprinkle with caster sugar if desired, and serve warm or cold.

Variations

As a shortcut, use ready-made sweet shortcrust pastry. Try sprinkling the finished pastries with chopped pistachios as well as, or instead of, sugar.

Raja, Kanak Durga

We are in one of Asha's many community centres, this time in Kanak Durga meeting Raja, who is the youngest person sharing a recipe with us. He is 17 years old and still in school but he impresses us with his quiet maturity. We hear how he has overcome many obstacles already.

Raja lives in a typical one-room home where space and light for studying is a barely affordable luxury. He is the main cook for his extended family of ten, which includes his mother, father, four brothers, sister-in-law and two sisters. Today he is making kheer. The milk bubbles away on the little gas stove as he talks us through the recipe. He enjoys being the family cook, so he is now taking a 'home science' class at school. Some of the Asha team members in the room are surprised to hear of boys studying this. Home science is traditionally a female-dominated subject, but Raja laughs and says that out that of the eleven students in his class, six are boys.

It's good to hear how he is finding a way forward for his future: as he describes his life, we can see where this strength has come from. Since before Raja was born, his mother has had a condition that causes her to have fits, and he says she cannot manage housework. Raja takes care of the household. He tells us that his father is a tailor for an export company on the far side of Mayapuri, but he spends all his money on alcohol. Raja works hard to look after the family while keeping up with his schoolwork. He wakes at 4.30am to do a paper round, delivering to 120 houses for an hour before school. From that job he earns 1200₹ a month (approximately £13), which pays for his school books, stationery and English lessons; the remainder he gives to his mother.

Ayesha is the staff member showing us around today and she tells us that Raja's family's prospects are really improving. His brother has trained as an electrician. His sister Rajini left school last year and was recently able to get a good job with a French-owned shoe company, after securing an initial placement with an Asha corporate supporter operating at Delhi airport. Ayesha gives us some context: 'For a while Raja and his siblings lived on chapattis and salt: they were very, very poor.' Raja's sights are now set on a hotel management, or on becoming a chef, and he is working out how to go to college. Although this is a new venture for him, he has positive role models and encouragement from his sister, brother and also his Asha family. They know how to guide him to fulfill his potential, and he has shown us that he has the aptitude to make it happen.

Paneer ki kheer

RAJA, HIGH SCHOOL STUDENT AT KANAK DURGA SLUM

Kheer, or rice pudding, is a very popular Indian dessert. Raja learnt this unusual version at school in home science, and now makes it at home on special occasions. It is one of a repertoire of dishes he cooks; when he leaves school he hopes to become a chef or go into hotel management. This kheer is made with grated paneer instead of rice, and as a result tastes particularly creamy. The fresh coconut and dried fruit offset the richness, and Raja explains that it can be served hot or cold. He smiles humbly as he offers us the kheer, which he has simply decorated with one or two almonds. It is delicious, and Raja undoubtedly has a bright future ahead of him.

SERVES 6

1 litre full-fat milk
500g paneer (Indian cheese), finely grated
½ fresh coconut, finely grated or 225g (or two snack pots) of fresh coconut chunks
150g of a mix of sultanas, raisins, cashew nut pieces, fresh coconut slivers
6–7 heaped tbsp sugar

Put the milk in a large pan and bring to the boil. Simmer for 30 minutes to reduce it slightly. Add the paneer, stirring constantly, until it is evenly blended throughout the liquid.

Add the grated coconut, dried fruit and nuts. Stir well, then add the sugar. Cook on a medium to high heat for 10–15 minutes until it is creamy and thickened. Serve hot, at room temperature or cold, garnished with additional fruit or nuts if desired. I like it served chilled or at room temperature with fresh mango or pineapple on the side.

Masala chai

DURGESH, ASHA COMPUTER TEACHER AT ZAKHIRA SLUM

I clearly remember my first cup of masala chai in India. I was painting an Asha centre and one of the ladies asked if I wanted chai. I knew that meant tea, but had no idea it meant tea infused with milk, sugar and aromatic spices. She handed me a tiny cup of steaming, fragrant liquid, and with one sip I was utterly sold. Durgesh's mother has had a chai shop in the slum for 28 years and this is her famous recipe, which Durgesh reverently prepared for us. Perfect after an Indian meal, restorative after a long winter's walk and comforting snuggled up in bed with a good book, this never disappoints.

SERVES 2–4

1 teacup of cold water
3 cloves
4 green cardamom pods
2–3cm slice of root ginger, bashed into 3–4 pieces
1 small cinnamon stick, broken into shards
Large pinch of fennel seeds
2 heaped tsp loose-leaf Assam tea (or 2 strong teabags)
1 teacup of milk
1–2 tsp sugar

Put the water in a pan with all the spices and bring to the boil. Add the tea and continue to boil, stirring well, letting the flavours infuse for 2–3 minutes.

Add the milk and sugar; simmer for 10 minutes on a medium heat. Strain out the spices and serve in two mugs or four small chai cups.

Variation:

Leave out the sugar if you prefer unsweetened tea.

Fruity almond milk

DHANPATI, ASHA STAFF MEMBER AT KUSUMPUR SLUM

Dhanpati learnt to make this nourishing, infused milk from her mother and says it is common where she comes from in Uttar Pradesh. Made in winter and served instead of chai in the morning, or to guests, it is also given to nursing mothers after delivery. She explained that it is served after the meal at weddings, which is poignant, as she tells us she was a child bride at five years old. She stayed at home until puberty, then moved to live with her husband when she was sixteen, having the first of her four children a year later. A huge smile lit up her face as she described how fulfilling she has found working for Asha for the last 14 years. Do give this unusual recipe a try. The result is comforting and delicious.

SERVES 6

25g almonds
25g cashew nuts
50g pitted dates, chopped
25g raisins
1 tbsp desiccated coconut
1 tbsp ghee or butter
Pinch ground turmeric
1 litre full-fat or semi-skimmed milk
5 green cardamom pods, bruised to split them open
4 tbsp caster sugar

Soak all the nuts and dried fruit, including the coconut, in cold water for two hours. Drain and grind to a smooth paste in a blender, adding a little of the milk if necessary. (If it is bitty at this stage, sieve out the lumps to give a smooth texture.)

Heat the ghee in a pan and fry the fruit-nut paste until it is light golden, adding the turmeric for extra colour. Set aside.

Put the milk in a large pan with the cardamom pods and bring to the boil. Turn the heat down and add the fruit-nut paste and the sugar. Stir well to dissolve the sugar and mix in the paste. Simmer for 5 minutes, remove the cardamom pods and serve warm in little espresso cups.

Ravinder, Kanak Durga

Ravinder has a sharp haircut and a wide smile. He tells us that he enjoyed an evening out with work friends just the day before, so he shows us in his easy-going way how to make one of his favourite non-alcoholic cocktails. However, he has another side: he has worked hard to make the most of the opportunities he has been given, and his successes are well earned. Two months ago he secured a job with a U.S. telecommunications company, handling the complex business of their refunds policy.

Just a few months earlier, Ravinder gained his BA in commerce. He explains that internships with global corporates arranged by Asha really helped him find a good job soon after graduating. Life is good and he has high expectations for himself

in the future. 'I want to work in a joint venture and I expect to continue my education too,' he says. 'I am learning new things every day.' He tells us that part of the fun of life now is getting to know his colleagues. 'My team members are like brothers. They are from all over India. Work is in English, but it's a Hindi office, so I'm learning their dialects.'

His real family members have each gained from Asha's support. His mother and two brothers all joined Asha groups, which meant they could access practical training, the encouragement of their peers, school support, loans, and become engaged citizens. Asha gave an MBA study loan to his older brother, who is now working in the food industry.

Ravinder is gratefully fulfilling Asha's belief in 'paying it forward' by volunteering with the younger generation. He works with the older Asha students in Kanak Durga who are in Class 12 or at university. It's a really intensive role, as Ravinder wants to pass on to them everything he has learned. 'I motivate them through workshops, which are typically attended by 15 students and I give specific classes to four or five students at a time. I try to help them with their resolve to continue in education. As Asha ambassadors we share whatever knowledge and skills we have. I know about accounting and commerce related subjects, so that's what I pass on.' He mentions that he works five days a week, and I ask him how often he comes to volunteer at the Asha centre. I'm humbled by his answer: 'Two days a week. I'm the only student ambassador in my slum.'

As we prepare to toast Ravinder's achievements and thank him for sharing his story with us, he adds a sprinkle of salt to each cup of citrus juice and soda. A breeze blows through the open door, carrying a good smell of fresh earth. 'When you add salt,' he noted, 'it makes bubbles.'

Citrus punch

RAVINDER, STUDENT AMBASSADOR AT KANAK DURGA SLUM

Ravinder took the day off from his international corporate job to meet us, tell us his story and serve us this refreshing soft drink. He tells us proudly that he learnt it at a bar whilst celebrating a colleague's birthday. He smiles as he admits that despite being a foodie, he doesn't cook, hence the choice of a drink as his contribution. Thirst-quenching on a warm day in Delhi, this family-friendly citrus drink would be great here at a BBQ, with some spicy fried chicken, or of course with a hot curry. Don't be tempted to skip the salt: it makes it very moreish and complements the sweetness of the fresh juices beautifully.

SERVES 4

250ml freshly squeezed or good
  quality orange juice
1 tbsp caster sugar
300ml Sprite
Juice of 1 large lemon
Juice of 1 large lime
¼ tsp salt
Ice cubes
Lemon or lime slices to garnish

Mix the orange juice with the sugar in a jug. Add in the freshly squeezed lemon and lime juice. Divide equally between 4 glasses and top up with the Sprite.

Stir a pinch of salt into each glass (which makes it bubble). Top up with ice cubes and decorate with a slice of fresh lemon or lime. Alternatively, just mix everything together in the jug and serve immediately.

Recipe index

Want to get involved?

FIND OUT MORE ABOUT ASHA

Take a look at the website and read in more detail about all that's going on in Delhi.

www.asha-india.org

If you'd like a copy of the monthly newsletter, register your interest by emailing foasha.richardhogben@gmail.com

DONATE TO HELP THEIR WORK!

If you are a UK taxpayer, you can Gift Aid your donation. Friends of Asha (GB) (Charity Registration No. 1085071) can collect an extra 25p for every pound you donate. Visit the Asha page below to download the gift aid form.

Donate online: go to https://asha-india.org/get-involved/donate/great-britain-donations

Donate by BACS: make payment to account name: Friends of Asha (GB); Lloyds Bank sort code 30-96-31 A/C No 01899891

HOST A CURRY NIGHT!

Invite your friends round, and cook up a storm! Choose your favourite recipes in the book and then gather friends and family to come and enjoy them with you or make it easier by hosting it in your local curry house. Either ask for a donation or pop a jam jar on the table to collect their contributions.

Every autumn, Friends of Asha (GB) promote the Big British Curry Night, where Asha supporters all over the UK are encouraged to host a Curry Night in October.

Check out details on Facebook via Asha Society or Friends of Asha (GB).

GET IN TOUCH

Find out more about this project at hopeandspice.com or email info@hopeandspice.com

Thank you...

Writing this book has been an enormous gift to us and we have many people we would like to thank, without whom we simply couldn't have done it. It has felt like a dream come true and we are so grateful for the opportunity to turn a little idea into a real project that has become this beautiful book. Our very heartfelt gratitude goes to:

• **Dr Kiran and Freddy Martin:** Thank you Kiran for saying 'yes' to the idea, and for the warmth and hospitality that you and Freddy extended to us when we stayed with you whilst researching the recipes. Thanks to Radha, Ujala and Santosh for their care, cooking and warm welcome-home smiles.

• **Ayesha and the office team:** Ayesha, your planning, encouraging, editing and proofreading has kept us on track and been so supportive. We couldn't have done it without you! Thanks to Shreya, Shabnam, Ved, Amitava and Anwesha for looking after us 'in the field'. We loved your company.

• **Asha staff:** thanks to Rani, Sweeta and all the Asha staff who spent time with us, sharing your work and passion for the slum communities. You are shining examples of compassion and love and we admire your dedication to the people you serve. Thanks also to Chandermohan for driving us around so expertly in the crazy Delhi traffic.

• **Our cooks:** thank you to everyone who cooked for us, whether your recipe ended up in the book or not. We loved watching and learning from you and then enjoying your delicious dishes. We know there is so much more for us to learn, but hope we have done justice to your culinary heritage and skill. Thank you for sharing your recipes so enthusiastically and generously.

• **Friends of Asha (GB):** thank you to the trustees, who caught the vision for this project and gave us their support throughout. Hopefully this is not the end of the Hope & Spice journey!

• **Peter Bishop:** Pete you brought this to life so beautifully and gave us your talent and time so incredibly generously. We cannot thank you enough

for that and for your endless patience and cheery 'can-do' attitude. It was a joy to know you love India as much as we do.

• **Steve Lee:** Thank you for all your wizardry with our photos. You edited them brilliantly and brought the slums, the cooks and the food to life with your expert eye. Thank you for your generosity and support throughout and especially on the shoot. A shout-out to Charlie Lee, and Jo Harris as well, for your help with the shoot and for letting us use the beautiful props.

• **Our recipe testers:** Thank you all for your help in road-testing the recipes and making sure they worked. We are so grateful for your support; the book is better for your contributions: Mandy Turner, Emma Dobson, Sue Walton, Teri-Anne Cavanagh, Greg and Silvia Inglis, Jessica Rayleigh, Sarah Dinsdale, Karen Jones, Brad Crampton, Libby Etherington, Nicky Hilyer, Christina Wood, Rachel Calvert-Lee, Sam Simpson, Ruth Wadey, Dave Cooke, Aideen Wallich, John Parrish, Gilly Charkham, Debbie Rycraft, Lindsey Solomons, Sue Harper, Zoe Moore, Prue Brand, Nadine Banerjee, Helen Chen, Ena Burgess, Tina English, Suzie Steele, Julie-nne Monahan, Olivia Malhotra, Maria Bailey and Mike and Pandi Stepan.

• **Nicola Sessions:** thank you for your help with publicity.

• **Janette Simpson:** thank you for the time you put into editing some of this and sorry it couldn't have been more. You shared in Amanda's Asha journey at the start and maybe we can go back together sometime?

• **Proofreaders:** Thank you to Marion Lewis, Tommy Clegg, Greg Inglis, Craig Melcher and Shammah Banerjee for your care and diligence.

• **Our friends:** a million thanks to our friends that have encouraged, supported and prayed for us. You know who you are and we are so grateful for your friendship and love.

• **Our husbands:** Tim and Jonathan we love you and thank you for all your support. You ate curry with us at times when you didn't always want to and helped us in immeasurable other ways.